The Love Key
How to Unlock Your Psychic Powers to Find True Love

The Love Key

*How to Unlock Your Psychic Powers
to Find True Love*

JOANNA SCOTT

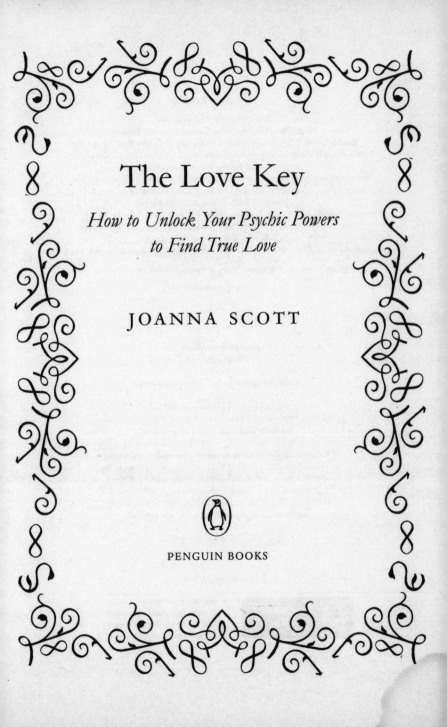

PENGUIN BOOKS

PENGUIN BOOKS

Published by the Penguin Group
Penguin Books Ltd, 80 Strand, London WC2R ORL, England
Penguin Group (USA) Inc., 375 Hudson Street, New York, New York 10014, USA
Penguin Group (Canada), 90 Eglinton Avenue East, Suite 700, Toronto, Ontario, Canada M4P 2Y3
(a division of Pearson Penguin Canada Inc.)
Penguin Ireland, 25 St Stephen's Green, Dublin 2, Ireland (a division of Penguin Books Ltd)
Penguin Group (Australia), 250 Camberwell Road, Camberwell, Victoria 3124, Australia
(a division of Pearson Australia Group Pty Ltd)
Penguin Books India Pvt Ltd, 11 Community Centre, Panchsheel Park, New Delhi – 110 017, India
Penguin Group (NZ), 67 Apollo Drive, Rosedale, Auckland 0632, New Zealand
(a division of Pearson New Zealand Ltd)
Penguin Books (South Africa) (Pty) Ltd, 24 Sturdee Avenue, Rosebank, Johannesburg 2196, South Africa

Penguin Books Ltd, Registered Offices: 80 Strand, London WC2R ORL, England

www.penguin.com

First published 2011
1

Set in 12.5/14.75 pt Garamond MT Std
Typeset by Palimpsest Book Production Limited, Falkirk, Stirlingshire
Printed in England by Clays Ltd, St Ives plc

ISBN: 978–0–241–95269–6

www.greenpenguin.co.uk

Mixed Sources
Product group from well-managed
forests and other controlled sources
www.fsc.org Cert no. SA-COC-1592
© 1996 Forest Stewardship Council

Penguin Books is committed to a sustainable future
for our business, our readers and our planet.
The book in your hands is made from paper
certified by the Forest Stewardship Council.

Contents

Introduction: Yes — You're Psychic

Did you know you can read minds? Yes, you really can. You may not consciously think you can, but believe me: you're a mind reader. We all are. Some of us have already fine-tuned our mind-reading abilities, which is why I, and others like me, work as professional psychics who give love advice to others. But we all have the gift of psychic power if we choose to use it, and this book is about bringing out your innate intuitive powers to answer the big questions you have about love. I wrote this book to help you, right now, to find true love and stop negative and destructive patterns in your dating experiences. I want to help end the horrible, reoccurring heartache many of us needlessly suffer when we don't use our psychic abilities to help us with our love lives.

So why did you pick up this book? As a psychic counsellor, I'm contacted every day by men and women seeking love advice. Do you need to heal a broken heart before you can move on, or do you want answers to dating and relationship questions? Many people contact me because they're hurting, and need to know where their relationship went wrong. But just as often, clients want to know more about someone they've just met or are just getting to know. Is he or she the right person for me? Is marriage on the cards? Is this person worth spending time with, or is there someone better for me out there?

Whatever questions you have about your love life,
you can use your psychic abilities to answer them.

The good news is, whether you've suffered a nasty break-up, are happily single or have just started a new relationship and need to know where it's going, this book will help you find all the answers you need. Once you've tuned into your psychic abilities, it's easy to find the answers. By mastering a few basic rules, strategies and patterns you'll learn to communicate directly with your intuition, or sixth sense, and answer every love question you've ever had. You may even experience powerful visions of love in the future.

You'll discover that 'psychic' abilities aren't as mysterious, magical or illogical as you may imagine, and that it's actually very easy to get in touch with your sixth sense and start seeing the world more clearly. As a matter of fact, you've almost certainly had psychic experiences already, but you perhaps haven't considered them in this way. All of us have had feelings about people that have been correct, yet we can't put our finger on why we felt the way we did. We often know when a partner is lying to us, even if every logical sign is to the contrary, and we also know when a date isn't interested – much as we like to tell ourselves this isn't so, then agonize over why he didn't call.

Once you've used this book to master your romantic psychic skills, you'll be able to mind read your dates and discover exactly how they feel about you and what's going on in their lives behind the scenes. You'll suss out the 'Mr Rights' and 'Mr Wrongs' right from the start by learning to see warning signs in your relationships before you're in too deep and experience that emotional pain. In fact, you'll start to look at potential partners in a totally different light, and know immediately if someone isn't right for you, or something about their initial behaviour doesn't quite add up.

> *You may think love is complicated, but when you look at life through your 'third eye' you'll see it's very simple indeed.*

And you'll learn more than just mind reading: you'll learn how to change your psychic energy to attract a loving, caring, sexy relationship that brings out the best in you and your partner. Instead of asking, 'Why didn't he call?', you'll be asking, 'Why am I so lucky?' And you'll learn how to change your energy so you stop repeating negative dating patterns.

I've spent ten years talking to heartbroken and confused women and men, and whilst helping them I've been given some amazing insights into relationships and love, including both the secrets of finding true love and the sure-fire routes to heartbreak.

One of the most astonishing things I've discovered is how often dating patterns repeat themselves, and how regularly I hear the same questions over and over again. So one of the first things you'll learn, as you develop your psychic abilities, is how to discover your love-life cycle. More than anything else, our love lives are an area where sensible people repeat the same negative patterns. Why? Because we're so used to living in a logical world, we ignore our inner wisdom, or intuition, and let ourselves

3

get stuck in the same bad relationship cycle. We listen to what people tell us, rather than using our psychic ability to feel their energy and thoughts. And the result? Confusion and heartache. When you get in touch with your sixth sense, you'll learn to break negative patterns, identify Mr Wrong before he breaks your heart and attract a loving partner who is absolutely perfect for you.

This book is also about sharing the experiences of the many people I've helped over the years, so you can learn from their mistakes – and, of course, their successes. During my years of psychic relationship counselling I've listened to thousands of love dilemmas, and as I share some of them with you, you'll almost certainly recognize experiences and relationship patterns in your own life.

Getting in touch with your psychic energy is exciting, and will help you make some incredible improvements in your love life.

I hope you're ready to get started. Everything in this book is simple and easy to understand, but some of the ideas may take some getting used to. Don't worry – with time and patience you'll get there and you will understand what is happening in your life today, as well as gaining an improved understanding of the past, and learning from it.

I promise this will be an exciting process, and you'll discover wonderful new things about yourself as you develop your abilities. You'll feel uplifted and eager to take action to make your love life better. But you may need to make some changes. You may need to take some

4

risks and look at your life, and yourself, in a very different way. Change can be a scary thing, but it is also very powerful. You only have to change a few small things, one or two habits and behaviours, and you'll find everything around you changes for the better. You may find yourself a very different person when you finish this book – don't say I didn't warn you!

So let's get started . . .

PART I
Your Secret Powers

Your Hidden Psychic Energy

Are you ready to start unlocking your psychic abilities? I believe everyone has intuition and psychic senses, but some of us have swept a clearer path to them than others. So we're going to begin clearing the path and building strong links with your innate psychic powers. I will teach you which voices belong to your inner wisdom and, perhaps most importantly, to *listen* to this intuition and wise guidance.

I've counselled hundreds of broken-hearted people, but I'm still frequently surprised by how often intuitive feelings are ignored. '*I knew something wasn't right from the start,*' my client will tell me, a month after her date has run off with her best friend. '*But I hoped for the best because I liked him so much.*' If only she'd listened to her inner wisdom. But, of course, many of us don't know the difference between our inner wisdom and the voice that arranges our shopping list. In this chapter you're going to practise getting in touch with your psychic side and listening to your higher self. Practice makes psychic, I always say. If you're sceptical about your own ability to hear a higher wisdom, or the concept of psychic abilities in general, all

I ask is that you try the exercises in this chapter for yourself. I promise you'll be pleasantly surprised by the results.

I'll teach you which voices belong to your intuition and, most importantly, how to listen.

When you're in tune with your psychic energy, you can foresee and prevent future relationship problems before they happen, you can see clearly who isn't right for you and understand exactly how to attract your soulmate, but building a strong link to your intuition doesn't happen overnight. It will take some work on your part. So we're going to begin with some warm-up exercises to train your intuitive brain and start unlocking your hidden psychic abilities. First, though, let me explain a little more about the rules I follow as a psychic, so you can begin to understand how to put your mind in the right place and start tuning into your powers.

My Five Psychic Rules

Every psychic works differently, but there are five simple rules I've found all good psychics follow. As long as you follow these rules and carry out the practices in this book, your psychic powers will grow and grow and you'll begin experiencing real miracles in your romantic and everyday life.

Rule One: Believe In Yourself

Self-belief is vital for psychic ability. The minute you begin to doubt yourself and your powers, your intuition stops talking to you. Believing in yourself is all about positive thinking – you must think positively about yourself and your abilities. I don't want you to think 'perhaps I can do this', or 'I'll try this and see what happens'. You must think 'I CAN DO THIS' and really, truly believe it.

Above all, don't be frightened. Fear can really get in the way of self-belief. Don't run away from situations that scare you – try them out, make mistakes if that's how it must be, learn and move forward. See fear as a good friend, helping you grow and improve.

Every day, do things that make you smile to make sure your positive energy is at maximum levels. What do you enjoy? Who makes you feel good? Take a trip away whenever you can to recharge your positive batteries and remind yourself how wonderful you really are. Trust yourself and trust that you are guided by something good and worthwhile.

Rule Two: Try to Keep the Peace Around Others

Unless you're feeling safe and comfortable, it's hard to invite the psychic world into your life. So it's very important to avoid conflict or aggressive behaviour with others. If you do find yourself at odds with someone, listen, learn and find ways to resolve things without resorting to anger. If you have unresolved hurt feelings, talk to the person concerned and reach a shared understanding for the future. Any friction or tension will block psychic energy and also prevent you from meditating and relaxing – another vital part of tuning into your intuition.

Rule Three: Only Use Psychic Abilities for the Highest Good

Your intuition is really your higher self, or the best side of you. Psychic insight is a gift, but not one that should be used for personal gain or selfish reasons. If you try to use your psychic abilities to take advantage of others, you will create a negative energy field around you that blocks your intuition. So please think long and carefully about what you intend to use your intuition for. Your intuition is there to help you, but your gain must never be at someone else's expense.

Rule Four: Relax, Relax, Relax

As you read this book I will teach you many different relaxation practices, and these will help you tune into your psychic abilities. Relaxation really is the key to connecting with your intuition. Top psychics are able to clear their minds and relax almost instantly. You'll find, if you ever meet a really good psychic, that they have an extremely calm and caring energy surrounding them. This is no accident – their ability to feel relaxed and loving at all times is part of what makes their intuition so powerful.

Your state of mind is very important when it comes to psychic abilities. The mind must be open and calm to let the right energy come through.

Rule Five: Practice Makes Psychic

We all know that good athletes and performers dedicate time and energy to training. If you want to be good at something, you have to be driven and motivated and put in the hours. My own psychic abilities didn't just happen overnight – I practised and practised, and learned about the many different ways psychics work, including reading cards, divination with crystals, aura reading and so on. I kept going, working on the abilities I already had until they were better and stronger and I could use them whenever I chose.

No one would take a driving test or an exam without practice and study. And it's the same with psychic work. You have to keep practising and never even think of giving up. With the right attitude, you'll find one magical day that miracles start to happen for you. You'll be able to read what others are thinking, ask for answers from your higher wisdom and predict the future.

Your psychic practice is about to begin. Are you ready?

Psychic Warm-Up

Don't let the idea of a warm-up worry you. It's simply my way of describing the first stage of psychic training, and I promise it will be lots of fun. Getting in touch with your intuition feels great, but it does take practice and effort, just like anything worthwhile. I've been lucky enough to have a connection with my psychic abilities from an early age, which means I've had more practice than most at using my intuition. But I'm here to tell you, *anyone* can hear their higher self, as long as they commit to regular practice. Even if you've never experienced strange coincidences, a 'funny feeling' pointing you in the right direction or a gentle voice telling you the right thing to do, I am confident what you are about to read will open up your inner psychic abilities. A psychic warm-up will help you tune in and listen carefully to the voice inside that always knows the right thing to do. But, remember, I can only show you the way. It's up to you to find time and practise.

Training Your Psychic Brain: the Basics

We're going to start the warm-up with a very important psychic exercise that will form the basis of your psychic training. Many psychics, including myself, use this exercise regularly to tune into our psychic powers. It's called the 'Psychic Staircase' and it's a great tool for meeting your psychic self, no matter what your current level of psychic expertise. The first thing you should do is find somewhere quiet and relaxing. If you're on a tube train on the way to work, sorry, that's no good. You'll need a nice quiet place, perhaps a bedroom or even a spiritual centre. The ideal spot is a beautiful, feminine space with nice fragrances, peaceful music and a comfortable sitting area where you can relax, undisturbed. But the most important thing is simply to find somewhere you can relax. Ready? Let's begin.

The Psychic Staircase

Important! Read this exercise all the way through before attempting it.

1. Find somewhere comfortable to sit, loosen any tight clothing and take a few deep breaths to settle your mind. Close your eyes.

2. Visualize a light, curved staircase leading downwards in a gentle spiral. The staircase has twenty steps, but the bottom steps are shrouded in swirling white cloud. Imagine the staircase any way you would like it to be, but know the steps are safe and shallow and easy to negotiate. You are at the top of the staircase looking down, and you are happy and excited about what you're going to find at the bottom. You feel a gentle, loving energy emanating from the bottom of the staircase.

3. You're now going to slowly walk down the steps. With each step, count downwards in your mind, starting from 20, so 20, 19, 18 . . . slowly going down the staircase. Whilst you're descending and counting quietly to yourself, repeat this sentence over and over in your mind: 'I am going deeper into a psychic level, deeper and deeper, slowly I go.' Feel safe, calm and relaxed. Take your time.

4. When you reach the bottom of the staircase, you'll feel the mist clearing and a tremendous feeling of peace

and calm. Say to yourself: 'I am now at a strong level of psychic awareness which will guide me and give me answers to my questions.' Say this slowly and with kindness. Repeat it as often as you need until you feel very calm and in tune with yourself. Then slowly open your eyes. What do you see? What do you hear and feel?

The first time you carry out this exercise, you might feel nothing more than just a sense of calm and well-being. If you were over-focusing on pinning down a psychic vision, you might have experienced a slight sense of panic or anxiety. Or you may have had a clear vision or thought that guided you in a positive direction. Everyone is different. Some of us see strong images when we're in touch with our higher selves, others hear voices, have a feeling about something or just suddenly 'know' the answer to an important question.

Your inner guide will answer all your dating questions and steer you towards your soulmate.

Whatever you experience, it's important not to worry or over-judge this exercise the first time you do it. Remember what I said at the beginning of this chapter? Practice makes psychic. You wouldn't expect to be able to play the flute after one lesson, or jump hedges on a horse without any practice at all, would you? This is the problem most people experience with psychic energy. They have a few tries, don't feel anything or experience anything unusual and decide, 'OK, it's me, I'm just not psychic.' But with practice and perseverance, I promise you'll experience some amazing insights into, not only your life, but the lives of your friends and family too. You'll find a wise inner guide that will help answer all your dating questions and steer you towards your soulmate.

Soon You'll Be Flying

I always start beginners with the Psychic Staircase exercise, but later you'll learn more psychic exercises that may be even more effective for your personality type. These include a flying visualization in Chapter 4 (which I call 'Sky Meditation') and a powerful anchoring technique in Chapter 13 that links your energy to the safety of the ground. With all these psychic tools available to you, soon your intuition will be flying high.

When you begin a period of psychic training, your friends and family will notice the difference in you. They might not be able to pinpoint quite what that difference is, but don't be surprised if you start hearing comments about how much more relaxed or focused you are, or how much clearer you seem about love and relationships. This is exciting. It means you're really tuning into your hidden psychic abilities. The more you practise, the less hidden and secret your abilities will be, and soon you'll be using them in daily life without even thinking about it.

2

Test Your Intuition – How Psychic Are You?

Now we've warmed up your psychic powers, I'd like to test your psychic abilities. We all have powers of clairvoyance, but I'd like you to discover just how in tune you already are with your powers of clairvoyance in your daily life and how much work you need to do to put your hidden powers to use. Once you've tested your psychic connection, we're going to go on psychic retreat, where those who need to can hone their intuitive powers further with daily exercises.

How Psychic Are You?

Ready to test your psychic abilities? This quiz will shed light on the most important relationship in your life – your relationship with your intuition. Answer the questions, choosing A, B or C depending on which response best describes you currently. The answer doesn't have to match your situation exactly – a good fit is good enough. You can calculate your score at the end.

Q1. When you meet someone for the first time, do you:

A · Just know whether you like them or not?

B · Go with the flow, don't judge and see what happens?

C · Look for concrete clues about what sort of person they are, such as how they dress or what they do for a living?

Answer A · *You're trusting your instincts, which means you're listening to your higher self and letting it work for you. Very often, your feelings about a person will be right. Score 3 points.*

Answer B · *You're open-minded, but try allowing your instincts to work harder. See what feelings come to you the next time you meet a new person. Score 2 points.*

Answer C · *You're allowing previous programming to cloud your intuition. Try keeping an open mind the next time you meet a new person, ignore anything logical you learn about them and listen to your feelings instead. Score 1 point.*

Q2. When the phone rings do you:

A · Just answer it as normal?

B · Often know who it will be and are usually correct?

C · Sometimes get a feeling about who it might be, but often get it wrong?

Answer A · *You aren't letting your instincts talk to you. The next time the phone rings, try and guess who's calling. This will help your psychic development. Score 1 point.*

Answer B · *If you often know when someone is going to call, you are strongly in touch with your psychic and telepathic talents. You have a good ability to tune into other people and their thoughts. Score 3 points.*

Answer C · *With more practice, you'll find you frequently know who is going to call. Keep guessing! Score 2 points.*

Q3. When someone you're dating promises to call but doesn't, do you:

A · Think up lots of reasons why he hasn't called, and go back and forth in your head the whole time, not sure what to believe?

B · Ask your friends why he hasn't called, and believe the nicest answer you hear?

C · Trust your first instinct to tell you why he hasn't called?

Answer A · *Your first thought was probably the right answer, but now you've buried this intuitive wisdom under a lot of logic and programming. Trust yourself more. Score 2 points.*

Answer B · *Asking friends about romantic situations is the best way to ignore your intuition. You're letting other people, who don't have the same intuitive sense of your situation, cloud your judgement and take responsibility for your love life. Remember – you know best! Score 1 point.*

Answer C · *Well done! I'm glad you trust yourself. Unless you're letting negative emotions rule your thinking, you'll almost certainly get the right answer. Score 3 points.*

Q4. When things go wrong for you, do you normally:

A · Do something that will take your mind off things?

B · Feel angry, depressed or lonely and often dwell on things for too long?

C · Try to relax and remain optimistic, and give yourself time to consider the situation in detail?

Answer A · *This approach is good as it keeps you relaxed, but by distracting yourself you may hold on to negative emotions that block your intuition or miss valuable life lessons. Score 2 points.*

Answer B · *By giving in to anger and negative emotions, you enter an emotional turmoil that clouds your intuition. Score 1 point.*

Answer C · *This approach is great for your intuition. Staying upbeat stops negativity damping down your psychic abilities, and the more relaxed you are, the more likely you'll hear intuitive wisdom and learn the right lessons. Score 3 points.*

Q5. When you are with a date/friend, do you ever know what they are going to say next?

A · You *are* joking? I don't even know what I'm going to say next half the time.

B · Very often. We sometimes finish off each other's sentences.

C · Sometimes, depending on where I am and what I'm feeling.

Answer A · *At least you're honest! Don't worry. By the time you've finished this book you'll have many intuitive skills that will enhance your relationships. Score 1 point.*

Answer B · *You're in touch with your psychic abilities, and have a potential soulmate in your friend/date, even if the situation isn't a romantic one. Score 3 points.*

Answer C · *This is a good answer, because you're aware of psychic processes and how to bring out the best in your conversations with others. Score 2 points.*

Q6. When you make a decision, do you stick with it or change your mind?

A · I try not to make decisions. I normally ask others to make them for me.

B · I'm forever changing my mind, then realizing I made a wrong choice.

C · I always go with my first choice as I trust my instincts.

Answer A · If you rely on others to make choices for you, you won't learn from your mistakes or move forward. Trust yourself more. I believe in you! Score 1 point.

Answer B · It's fine to change your mind, as long as you're going on instinct rather than fear. If you often change your mind and end up making the wrong decision, chances are your gut instinct was overridden by panic. Score 2 points.

Answer C · It's great to trust your instincts. They'll always take you to the right place, even if the route isn't immediately obvious. Score 3 points.

Q7. Imagine you're walking or driving in a new town, and you're lost. Do you:

A · Take a guess about which direction to take, but know you'll most likely need to ask for directions at some point.

B · Follow your instincts and head straight where you think you need to go. You know you'll find your way eventually.

C · Get the sat nav or map out (now where did I put it?), or immediately ask for directions.

Answer A · *Were you really trusting your instincts? Or panicking and taking a wild guess? Try to listen to yourself a little more. The next time you get lost, before you ask for directions take some deep breaths and ask your higher self for guidance. Score 2 points.*

Answer B · *I've often tested my instincts whilst lost and just thought: 'OK, let's try this direction and see where it leads me.' Nine times out of ten, I get where I need to go and often discover something interesting along the way. So well done for trusting your instincts. Score 3 points.*

Answer C · *You're not listening to your intuition, but I understand why. Getting lost is stressful! Be brave next time and just try the first direction that comes to you. You can always pull the map out afterwards. Score 1 point.*

Q8. When you sleep, do you:

A · Rarely or never have memorable dreams?

B · Occasionally have dreams, not always in colour and not always detailed?

C · Dream very deeply, with colours and images, and often these dreams match real life?

Answer A · *Dreams are an excellent source of psychic material, so if you don't remember your dreams you're missing out. Before you go to sleep at night, try asking your dreams to be more memorable. It sounds strange, but it works! Score 1 point.*

Answer B · *Your thoughts and intuitions are strong, but more practice is needed. By the time you've finished reading this book, you'll be dreaming in more detail and gaining useful insights. Score 2 points.*

Answer C · *People with strong psychic abilities have very detailed dreams, and sometimes sleep premonitions which come true in real life. You may even gain messages and information from your dreams if you look out for them. Lucky you! Score 3 points.*

Q9. Do you know what you are going to do tomorrow?

A · Yes, I know exactly. Circumstances beyond my control may change things, but I generally know what I'm doing from one day to the next.

B · Sorry, what day is it? I have no idea what I'm doing tomorrow.

C · I know roughly and I can sort of picture it, but I don't plan.

Answer A · Focus is good, but if you focus too hard you won't leave any room for your intuition. Try leaving things more open tomorrow, and see if you learn anything interesting or useful. Score 2 points.

Answer B · Do you feel life is getting on top of you right now? You'll feel much calmer if you take a little control of your life by visualizing and thinking ahead. Calmness is vital for tuning into psychic energy. Score 1 point.

Answer C · You have a good balance between visualizing and letting the day take you. Visualizing tomorrow helps the day go where you want it to go. Score 3 points.

Q10. Think of the last person you dated or had romantic feelings for. Do you know how they feel about you?

A · I really have no idea.

B · I think I know, but sometimes I think the complete opposite. It's confusing!

C · I feel I have a very clear understanding of them and their feelings towards me.

Answer A · Search deeper into your feelings. You do know. The answer is there. You just have to get in touch with it. Score 1 point.

Answer B · *I understand your confusion. Sometimes your intuition is there for you, but sometimes you let it get clouded by either what you want to think, or by logic judgements that result from previous programming. Trust your intuition, no matter what answer it gives you, positive or negative. Score 2 points.*

Answer C · *You're trusting your intuition and this is great. This means you're calmer and more self-assured in romantic situations, and better able to judge what's actually going on. Score 3 points.*

Q11. Do you believe in cosmic ordering, the law of attraction and what you project out you get back?

A · Yes, I really do. I've seen these concepts proved many times.

B · I believe that sort of thing is all a load of rubbish, just like the tooth fairy!

C · Sometimes, when life is going well.

Answer A · *This answer suggests you're very open to concepts that don't have a logical explanation, which is excellent. Being open-minded is the first step to trusting and listening to your intuition. Score 3 points.*

Answer B · *I can understand where you're coming from. But if you're to progress with your psychic abilities, I need you to free yourself from only believing in what can be* touched, seen and heard, and consider there may be more out there. *Score 1 point.*

Answer C · *This is a very typical answer, and makes complete sense. When you're happy and relaxed, you're more in touch with your intuition and therefore the world works with you. If you haven't had sufficient psychic practice, when life doesn't go your way, you'll let this affect your mood and consequently your belief system. Score 2 points.*

Q12. When you look at the clouds, do you:

A · Sometimes see shapes and pictures?

B · Just see a cloud?

C · See clear images that convey messages to you?

Answer A · *This is a good answer, as you have an ability to visualize and see more than just what your eyes tell you. This talent will help you carry out some of my powerful visualization techniques that will draw the perfect person towards you. Score 2 points.*

Answer B · *Next time you look at the clouds, get yourself in a relaxed state of mind and let them speak to you. Don't worry if you don't see anything straight away. Just watch them changing until an image appears. Score 1 point.*

Answer C · *Like crystal balls, clouds are an excellent way of clearing your mind and freeing your subconscious. You* *have a good ability to let your subconscious talk to you, so keep looking out for those images and messages. Score 3 points.*

How Did You Score?

12–18 points: *Psychic Beginner*

You're new to psychic learning, but that's fine. Often people with the least experience learn the quickest once they open the door. Perhaps you're a little sceptical about the idea of psychic powers, or have been treated badly in the past and find it hard to trust yourself. I often find negative past experiences and low self-esteem are the biggest hindrances to intuition, so we're going to work on these issues throughout the book. Because you're just beginning to learn about your psychic powers, you'll be particularly excited by the talents you discover as we progress together. Get ready for a wonderful journey.

19–26 points: *Psychic Intermediate*

You've already got an understanding of your psychic abilities, but you're not able to control them or make them work when you want them to. Often, you're not sure of the difference between your intuitive higher self and conscious logical programming. It can be difficult, without knowledge or practice, to hear your higher self. But you're not alone. Learning to differentiate is difficult without the right tools, and you're certainly not given these tools at school. Luckily, you're holding in your hands many psychic tools that will help you tune into your powers and help you really *hear* intuitive messages.

27–36 points: Psychic Goddess

You have a very strong connection with your psychic abilities and use them regularly to guide you throughout life. From a young age, you've had a good ability to assess people and situations, and have sometimes predicted events before they happened. You may work in the psychic industry, or a profession that uses your ability to tune into the feelings of others, such as teaching, marketing or counselling. However, romance evokes strong feelings that can cloud even the most intuitive person, so most likely you've chosen this book to help you work through negative feelings and hone your psychic abilities in the area of relationships.

So how did you do? If you're a beginner or intermediate psychic, hold on to your crystal ball because you're about to train hard and unleash abilities you'll be absolutely astonished by. If you're already a psychic goddess and intimately connected with your psychic abilities, think of the following exercises as toning and revitalizing. They'll keep your psychic powers in shape, but you needn't complete the full programme unless you want to. However, the rest of the book will certainly help you boost your powers of attraction and use your intuition in the sphere of relationships. Use your intuition as a guide, and remember, even the best of us can pick up new tips for tuning in. Psychic energy can be slippery. Sometimes it's elusive, even for professional psychics like myself, and new techniques can free you from a psychic block.

3

Take Your Mind on Psychic Retreat

I'm now going to ask for a three-week commitment to psychic training, which I call 'psychic retreat' and includes a 'psychic weigh-in' once a week. However, if the 'How Psychic Are You?' quiz revealed you were a psychic goddess, you probably don't need to go on psychic retreat for a full three weeks. Take a look at the retreat schedule and the psychic weigh-in, then choose whichever elements you feel will be useful.

If you were a beginner or intermediate psychic, on the other hand, I absolutely insist that you commit to a three-week retreat. When those three weeks are up, you'll see some amazing developments in your psychic self. But don't worry. Retreat or not, I won't ban you from watching television or have you waking at 5 a.m. to meditate. What I'd like you to do is follow this simple week-by-week schedule:

Psychic Retreat Schedule

Important! When you've finished reading about your three-week schedule, read the 'Psychic Weigh-In' section before beginning your three-week retreat.

Week 1: Repeat the Psychic Staircase exercise every day, preferably first thing in the morning as soon as you wake up. Write down any thoughts, feelings or visions you have in a notebook after you do the exercise.

Week 2: Repeat the Psychic Staircase exercise every other day (four times in total), again preferably first thing in the morning, but this time keep your eyes open whilst you carry out the exercise. Write down any thoughts etc. in a notebook.

Week 3: Check your notebook. Which days of the week did you have your best insights? Choose two of your best days (for example, Tuesday and Sunday) and this week carry out the Psychic Staircase exercise on these days. There's no need to record your revelations – just try to remember anything worthwhile.

After the three weeks are up, you may practise the exercise once a week (but no more than that) to keep your psychic energies buzzing. I promise that each and every one of you will reveal at least two important and useful insights about your current romantic situation, and probably many more. I also promise you *will* find your intuition grows stronger the more you carry out this exercise. The more you practise, the quicker images and feelings will come to you too, and you'll feel much more certain about what you're seeing and experiencing.

I promise your intuition will grow stronger during your three-week retreat.

The Psychic Weigh-In

It's good to see how far you're progressing when you learn a new skill, and psychic abilities are no different. Often, when people try to boost their intuition they don't measure their progress, which means they get bored of practising and soon don't bother. Which means their powerful psychic abilities aren't used. What a waste! So here is an exercise to help you test your psychic progression.

Ready for your weigh-in? During your three-week retreat, I'd like you to weigh your psychic abilities at the end of each week to see how well you're doing and to help free your unconscious mind. I have a set of simple questions I'd like you to answer – twice. The first time, I'd like you to answer the questions by thinking things over logically and coming up with the answer that best fits. The second time, I'd like you to go through the Psychic Staircase exercise, remain in your comfortable, peaceful place with a clear mind and let your intuition answer the questions for you. Use a pen and paper to write down your answers. You'll generally find the questions much easier to answer the second time around – just write down the first thought that comes into your head, even if it doesn't feel like it makes sense at first. Ready for the questions? Here we go.

1. What do you love about yourself?
2. Why are you not in a happy relationship?
3. What would your dream relationship look like?
4. How would you achieve this perfect relationship?

You'll more than likely see a real difference between the two sets of answers, but don't worry if you don't at first. The whole point of this exercise is to chart your progression, so when you repeat it during your three weeks of training, you're likely to find some different revelations coming to the surface as you get closer to your psychic powers. Your conscious mind has a set of beliefs and limitations that you exercise without even realizing it, and it takes practice to let go of existing ideas and assumptions. By checking your progress and 'weighing in', you're helping free yourself from unconscious restraints and clearing a pathway to your higher power. Get ready for some exciting results.

Detox Your Mind

Negative energy is the number-one block when it comes to connecting with your intuition and psychic powers. Bad energy and emotions are problems for all of us, from psychic beginners to professionals. We all get bogged down by bad vibes from time-to-time, so learning to regularly clear negative energy is hugely beneficial and will really cleanse your mind and set you on the right path for relationship wisdom. Together we're going to work on detoxifying your mind and breaking down bad habits. You'll feel much lighter and happier after a mind detox, which will clear negative energy and open up your psychic powers. Later on in the book, we'll work on specifically freeing you from the negative energy of past relationships, but for now we're just going to do a general clearing to get rid of current negative clutter.

What causes negative energy? Negative thoughts. We all have them. Even the most spiritual among us get flooded with negative emotions sometimes, and there's no shame in feeling hurt, angry, jealous, fearful or insecure. There's nothing wrong with these emotions. They're human emotions and you're a human being. Feelings are there to teach us things and without them we'd be emotionally lost. The problem comes when we *hold on to* these feelings for longer than we should and allow them to block our emotional progress. So I'm going to teach you how to identify and let go of these nasty negatives that shout so loudly and block your intuition and your natural wisdom.

> *Once you understand your negative emotions, you can build a true path to your higher psychic abilities.*

The first stage on this journey is to identify any bad emotions swirling around your consciousness right now. We'll decide what their purpose is and what they can teach you. Then we'll work on clearing them away. Once you understand your negative emotions, you can build a true path to your higher psychic abilities and get some firm answers about your relationships.

What are your key negative nasties? What are the dominant negative emotions in your life when it comes to relationships? Anger? Self-pity? Jealousy? Insecurity? Fear? Most people will experience a mixture of these emotions during a bad relationship, but we all have a few dominant negative emotions – the ones we turn to most of the time. Even without using your intuition, you're probably already aware of the negative emotions that dominate your life when things aren't going the right way. If you're really not sure, ask a family member or close friend. It's amazing how easily people can identify negative behaviour in themselves or others, but how difficult many of us find it to trust our inner wisdom and intuition! I want you to be really honest about your negative nasties. No hiding away. The only shame in experiencing negative emotions is not identifying and acting on them.

Please be warned, though, that if you ask someone you trust about your negative nasties, you may at first be quite shocked by what they say. Ask more than one person, just to get a clear picture, but be very certain those people are very trustworthy with your emotions. Once you've listened to a few friends, you may want to make a list of what *you* think your negative nasties are, alongside the friendly feedback you've received, and see if anything overlaps. Ultimately, you have to decide for yourself what seems most true and fits your personality best.

Now we need to discover what these nasties are trying to teach you. We tend to hang on to negative emotions because we're pulling against the lesson they're trying to communicate. Usually that lesson is an important revelation about ourselves and our own behaviour, *not* the behaviour of a partner. The strongest negative emotions are usually *misplaced* emotions. Why? Because when we misplace emotions, by resenting our ex, the woman he was unfaithful with, his family who were so rude and so on, we're looking for the lesson in the wrong places. And that means we'll never learn. So the nasty emotions stay until we *do* learn.

> *Until you take responsibility for past relationships,*
> *you'll be stuck with negative feelings.*

The truth is, YOU are responsible for your relationships. You chose your partner. So negative emotions will generally show you how *you* could have prevented the bad relationship you've just had to endure. If you've been abused, used and generally treated badly in a relationship, it doesn't mean you're not entitled to plenty of sympathy, and nor does it mean that your ex was a saint who didn't put a foot wrong. But the point is, until you recognize the role you played in bringing your relationship about you'll be stuck with emotions like anger, jealousy, self-pity, and all those other nasty feelings that make us feel bad and stop us moving on.

The Blame Game

It's time to take responsibility. You can no longer blame your ex for negative nasties, no matter how badly you were treated. To clear negative emotions, you have to take responsibility for your relationship and the warning signs you ignored. That's right: IGNORED. Because in every bad relationship there are warning signs, intuitive signals from your higher wisdom that shouted: 'I love you! Please stop here, or you'll get hurt!' Psychic energy is at its strongest when it's trying to help you, but so many people ignore or explain away intuitive warning signs. For many of us, it's second nature.

Do any of these thought processes sound familiar?

I have a bad feeling because he didn't call for a week. But he was probably busy with work. And he took me to a really expensive restaurant so I must mean something to him.

He really is behaving strangely. Is he hiding something? No, I'm probably being paranoid. Anyway [whispered], I don't want to probe too deeply, I might not like the answer.

If you've explained away your intuition with logic, only to discover that your intuition was right all along, don't worry. We've all done it – even me, and I'm a psychic counsellor! Human beings are romantic souls and we want relationships to work out, so we go about ignoring and covering up all the warning signs. Then we get hurt. And then we *think* we feel negatively towards our ex, when really those negative emotions are towards ourselves and our own behaviour. Or, more specifically, our own failure to protect ourselves.

Can you accept that you must take responsibility for any bad relationships you've experienced? If this sounds unfair, remember there were psychic warning signs (there are always warning signs) that you ignored. So although you may not have acted badly in the relationship, you at the very least didn't protect yourself by listening to the warning signs. And, finally, can you accept that, no matter how much you think you dislike your ex, you don't really feel negativity towards him at all? Really, you feel negativity towards yourself. Are you ready to accept these things? Good. Because once you accept you can move on, and those unpleasant, uncomfortable negative feelings will stop blocking your intuition and dominating your relationships.

> *Tell your higher self: 'I'm ready to leave negative emotions behind and I forgive myself.'*

It's time now to take a brave step. I would like you to say out loud the following sentence:

'I let myself get hurt. But I have learned my lesson. I am ready to leave negative emotions behind me. And I FORGIVE MYSELF.'

You're talking directly to your higher self when you say these words, and your higher self will listen.

Let's say those last words again. 'I FORGIVE MYSELF.' This is very important, because those negative nasties are strong signs that you *haven't* yet forgiven yourself. We all make mistakes. But now you've learned your lesson and you're not going to repeat the same mistake again. So you're ready to move on and you've taken a powerful step in unblocking your psychic energy and letting your intuition find you a kind, loving partner who is perfect for you.

You can repeat this process as many times as you like.

The more often you repeat positive sentences in your mind, the more chance they have of sinking into your subconscious and staying there. The more you repeat, the more your mind will focus on new, positive patterns, so remind yourself daily, weekly or whenever you feel your mind is steering off course.

How Anne's Negativity Ruled Her Relationships

Anne's last two relationships ended because of infidelity. On both occasions she felt utterly shocked and confused when she discovered her partner was having an affair. She couldn't believe she'd been so unlucky twice and felt overwhelming anger towards her last partner in particular. Whenever she thought about him, or the woman he'd been seeing behind her back, she felt a simmering rage that showed no signs of going away, even years later.

A quiet and well-spoken woman, Anne didn't voice her anger directly or talk about her past relationships to anyone except me, but her suppressed anger was so powerful it really was affecting her life in all sorts of negative ways. Without realizing it, she was creating a field of negative energy around her that was touching everyone she came into contact with.

During our first sessions together, Anne and I identified that she was angry (which brought huge relief and tears) and used tarot cards to pinpoint the lessons the anger was trying to teach her. In Anne's case, she'd known something had been wrong in her last relationship for many months before she had the courage to check her partner's phone, and it was this 'ostrich' behaviour that was the root of her anger. Deep down, she was furious with herself for making the same mistake twice and letting herself get hurt. Having resolved never to ignore relationship danger signs again, we worked on turning her anger into positive energy to clear a path to her intuition.

Clearing the Negative Clutter

The painful part is over. You've accepted responsibility for the pain you've experienced and the negative emotions you've been feeling. Now it's time to clear everything out. You may be expecting me to ask you to flood yourself with negative feelings in order to clear them out, but all that will do is increase your negative energy. What we're actually going to do is flood you with positive energy, which will drive a clear path to your intuition and have you on great speaking terms with your inner wisdom and psychic powers. Positive energy and intuition are best friends. So this is a very simple exercise to strengthen your positive feelings and make you feel great. It will take you around five minutes, but I've seen this exercise clear years of negative feelings.

The Power of Positive Energy

1. Write down any negative feelings you have about past relationships (for example: anger, resentment, jealousy, irritation, worry, insecurity, etc.).

2. For every negative emotion, write a positive benefit. For example, if you feel jealousy towards your ex and his new partner, you might write: 'This jealousy pushes me to find a relationship of my own.' Or if you feel insecurity about the way you've been treated in the past, you might write: 'Feeling insecure tells me I need to work on my self-confidence and find ways to feel better about myself.'

3. Thank the negative emotion for what it's giving you, then tell it you no longer need it any more. Smile and feel lightness and clarity.

Even if you don't feel light and clear-headed straight away, don't worry. This exercise is already doing wonders to loosen and release any negative energy and generate the happy, positive feelings your intuition loves. It is talking to your higher self to detoxify your mind. Mind detoxes are useful to carry out every six months or so, or whenever you feel a surge of negativity. Trust them to work for you and they will.

You've put in lots of hard work in this chapter, and really begun to unlock your psychic potential and get in touch with that inner voice that will guide you through even the trickiest of relationship trials. Commend yourself for your good work, but there's more to come yet!

4

Powering Up Your Intuition

We're now going to work on powering up your intuition and really strengthening your psychic abilities so they'll work both when you call upon them, and as you go about your daily life. Working with your intuitive feelings isn't about developing a new skill. It's about building an even stronger relationship with the psychic self that is already inside you. Men and women are equally intuitive so there's no reason to believe, if you're a man, that you'll have a harder time developing your intuition. But male or female, you should be prepared to spend some time working with your psychic self if you want to see results. I will promise you this, though: make just a little effort and you will be rewarded tenfold with insights and wisdoms that guide you, keep you safe and bring you love.

The Secret of Professional Psychics

I'm going to share with you now the key secret to strengthening your intuition and the psychic self. It is a secret all psychic professionals know and something most of us use every day to get in touch with our instincts. It is simply this: clearing the mind.

Most people think too much. Often, our minds are filled with daily chores, worries, problems, ideas . . . all sorts of things. Sometimes we're stressed or angry or tired. Life can be full of distractions, not to mention responsibilities and jobs to do. When our mind is ticking over all these niggly thoughts and concerns, we're about as far away from our intuition as we can be and as a result we make bad decisions – particularly when it comes to relationships.

Unlike the stressful or logical thoughts that demand our attention throughout the day, intuitive thoughts float quietly into the mind and don't require any further thinking. They are the solutions, not the problems. There is nothing difficult or stressful about intuition, which is why the calmer you are and the clearer your mind is, the easier it will be to relate to your intuition and consequently your psychic abilities. Trying to pull intuitive thoughts into your head doesn't work – you have to be calm and let them come.

During your psychic retreat you practised breathing deeply, calming down and tuning in. This is a great way to begin accessing your psychic powers as feeling relaxed and emptying the mind is the very foundation of psychic abilities. All intuitive thought comes from a calm place, which is why psychic professionals like myself all have our own various meditative, tuning-in techniques that help us clear our minds and feel calm and relaxed. I'm going to show you the technique I use regularly to clear my mind, and it works for me even when I've listened to many stressed or unhappy clients all day long. You may already have techniques and tricks you use to let go of conscious thoughts. Feel free to use these, and indeed be on the look-out for new mind-clearing ideas that suit you and your personality. But, for now, you can use the technique I enjoy to help clear my mind during my busy psychic practice.

Sky Meditation

This is a technique I use every day to put me in a calm state and help me meet my intuitive self. It is called 'Sky Meditation', and I use it before personal readings and also before I work on television and use my tarot cards live on air. It is a technique which is cumulative, by which I mean the more you do it the easier it becomes and the more effective it is. Sky Meditation is similar to the Psychic Staircase technique and in many ways the two techniques are interchangeable, but whereas the Psychic Staircase is a good warm-up and beginner exercise, Sky Meditation is more suited to clearing the mind when you're on the move and need to gain insight quickly, such as at work or whilst travelling.

The more you use this technique, or really any meditative clearing technique, the stronger your relationship with your intuition will be. You'll begin to experience amazing insights into the world around you and images will appear, both in dreams and real life, that guide you in a very positive way. Let me talk you though the Sky Meditation technique. Read through the technique once before attempting it.

1. Find a quiet, comfortable spot, perhaps a cushioned chair, comfortable sofa or bench outdoors.

2. Close your eyes.

3. Take a deep breath in, counting to seven as you do so, hold the breath for a count of three and then breathe out, again counting to seven. Continue breathing deeply but steadily.

4. As you breathe in, imagine cool, clear white air flowing into your mind and clearing away any words and images. The air is so white it covers any existing ideas, thoughts or pictures in your head like a summer cloud.

5. As you breathe out, imagine breathing away any thoughts, ideas, problems, pictures and really anything in your head along with the white air. If you find yourself thinking or getting distracted, imagine those thoughts getting tangled up in the white air and simply leaving your mind.

6. Keep breathing steadily, letting the air cleanse your mind. As the cleansing continues, imagine large white wings growing on either side of your head just above your ears. The wings get bigger and bigger and begin to flap, pulling you up towards the sky.

7. Imagine yourself flying in the clouds, higher and higher, your mind clear and your breathing deep.

8. Say to yourself: 'Please help me meet my intuition, with love, light and protection.'

You'll feel something of a shift in consciousness. Some people feel a rush of love or excitement, others feel serene and full of wisdom. Words and images will come to you now. Let them come and pay attention.

Not everyone has success with this technique first time. A few lucky people do tune in straight away, but most will find they need to practise the exercise a few times before it becomes really effective. As you begin using this technique, your first successes will mostly come down to how calm your mind is and your state of relaxation when you start the exercise. But the more you practise, the more you'll find that the technique itself will relax you and insights come even when you aren't feeling all that calm to begin with. Some people see images when their intuition starts talking to them, others see flashes or pictures or words, and some just suddenly 'know' something about a situation or have a feeling.

As you practise Sky Meditation and your intuition gets stronger, you'll start seeing clearer pictures and experiencing stronger feelings. The most common way strong psychic thoughts manifest are, believe it or not, through what many psychics describe as a little 'TV screen' in the mind. This 'TV screen' has been described in all sorts of different ways – as a moving picture box, a series of images, bright photographs, loud voices with pictures and so on – and the first time you see it can be quite alarming and disconcerting as it feels like something is coming in from 'outside' of you. But once you see strong, clear images like this you'll know you're really on the right path and building an excellent relationship with your psychic self.

Even if you don't see a 'psychic showreel' for a little while, you're still building a valuable relationship with your intuition and higher wisdom, and I promise this technique will be life-changing if you stick with it.

Boosting Psychic Powers Day by Day

Feeling calm is vital for tapping in to intuitive energy, but your intuition is with you all the time, throughout the day and night, and is always trying to communicate with you whether you're relaxed or not. I want you to get into the habit of listening out for those messages that come from your higher self because the more you pay attention, the stronger your bond with your psychic self will become and the more regularly your intuition will communicate with you. The key is, first and foremost, to be open. Some people simply refuse to believe that their intuitive side has wisdom to bring them, and this attitude of defiance works as a major block. If you're open to the possibility that your intuitive side has messages to give you and you look out for them as your day progresses, you'll find your psychic abilities grow rapidly. How might intuitive messages come to you as you go about your life?

Dreams

Intuitive thoughts often come to us in dreams. In fact, dreams can be one of the easiest ways to experience your intuition as a beginner, because when you sleep you can't help but let go of your logical self and let your psychic side communicate with you. The trouble with dreams is that sometimes it's difficult to relate the messages you get to real life, and dream messages can also be very forgettable when you wake up. Keeping a notepad by your bed is a good idea as you can jot down any dream thoughts and images and let your intuition mull them over. The dream messages will become clearer to you as the day progresses.

Coincidences

Look out for coincidences and serendipity, as these seemingly 'random' occurrences are often your intuition trying to get your attention. If a friend rings and you think to yourself, 'How strange – I was just about to call her,' pay attention to the phone call as it may have important information for you. If you find yourself taking an unusual route home and bump into an old friend on the way, be sure to take their details and keep in touch. Your intuition is trying to make something happen for you.

Feelings

If you feel happy or sad, upbeat or sluggish, calm or anxious, pay attention to these feelings. Don't try to suppress negative feelings with an extra cup of coffee or a 'cheer you up' chocolate bar – listen to them and understand what they're trying to tell you. What do you need to change? As for positive feelings – what's working well in your life and how can you make sure it continues?

Your Body

A good relationship with your body is vital as the body is often the way our intuition tries to communicate. Most of the time, we don't listen to our bodies. If we have a headache, we take a painkiller. If our skin itches, we rub ointment on to it. But we rarely listen to the messages our bodies are trying to tell us. Aches and pains, back problems, frequent colds, headaches and so on are all warning signs. They are your intuition telling you something is wrong in your life, either health-wise or emotionally.

I often come across clients who ignore their intuition and have reoccurring illnesses as a result. Sometimes these illnesses are the direct result of a bad relationship that is quite literally making them sick. How often have you heard people say things like, 'He makes me sick to my stomach,' or, 'She gives me a headache'? These phrases are usually light-hearted enough but they come from a serious place. A relationship that is full of conflict really can lower your immunity and make you ill.

As you go through the day, listen to what your body is saying because, more often than not, any aches and pains will relate to an emotional problem. On the flip side, if you feel great in certain situations and around certain people, this is a very positive message from your intuition that things are going well and you're on the right path.

So be aware that your intuition uses many methods to try and talk to you, even when you're not listening out for it, but it's also important to know that most of us have strong surges of psychic feelings at specific times of the day. We've all heard of the 'body clock', our internal clock that tells us when to eat and when to go to bed. But did you know you also have a psychic clock? Everyone's intuition works differently, and you may feel much more in tune with your psychic energy in the afternoon, late at night, or even on specific days of the week. Some psychic practitioners have their most profound thoughts first thing in the morning and have been known to stay under their duvets until their intuition answers their questions, and others prefer asking for guidance in the evening. Pay attention to the most intuitive times of days for you and work with them, especially when you're just beginning to build a relationship with your intuition. As time progresses, you'll find it easier to call upon your psychic abilities as and when you need them.

And now, a final word about building a strong relationship with your intuition. When your intuition talks to you, whether it's to give you an uneasy feeling on a date or send you a dream message about attending a party, pay attention and act accordingly. Doing so will build trust with your higher self and really strengthen your psychic abilities. It takes courage to act on intuitive feelings, but the more you do so the more your intuition will bring you guidance.

Talking to Your Psychic Self

Now I've shown you some techniques for powering up your intuition, I would like you to speak directly to your psychic self. I'm going to ask you some questions and you're going to use your intuition to answer. Before I give you the questions, I want you to clearly picture two colours in your head: red and green, just like a simple traffic light. Read the questions and let either red or green flash inside your mind. Red means 'no' and green means 'yes'. The colour you see in your head will answer the question.

If you hesitate too much on a single question, you may not be ready to make a decision there yet and that's fine. Come back to it at a different time. If you hesitate before many of the questions, make sure you're calm and maybe carry out the Psychic Staircase or Sky Meditation exercise before reviewing the questions again.

A good way to test you're in the right frame of mind to answer intuitive questions is to ask yourself a 'yes/no' question you already know the answer to, such as 'Am I a Capricorn?' or 'Do I own a car?' Wait for either red or green to flash up and if the colour is correct you'll know your intuition is in a good place.

You may also find it helpful to make two large circles, one coloured green with 'yes' written on it, and the other coloured red with the word 'no' written on it. When you ask the questions, feel which circle you're more drawn towards. Visual aids like this make it easier if you have a hard time picturing clear colours in your head.

Ready for the questions?

Questions For Your Psychic Self

These questions are designed to really get in touch with your deeper issues and feelings, the things you keep hidden from yourself and your logical mind. Some of you might experience a little discomfort as your intuition reveals things that your logical side may prefer to keep buried. But be brave and when you read the questions let go of conscious thought and allow your intuition to flash green for 'yes' and red for 'no'.

Get yourself in a calm place, breathe deeply and answer the following questions:

- Do you want to move house?

- Is your soulmate someone you already know?

- Do you want another job?

- Do you feel your family is proud of you?

- Do you feel good about yourself?

- Are you ready to live with a partner?

- Do you want to travel this year?

- Do you need to be single for a while?

This game can be a little scary, especially when you really feel the answers to be true. If you don't 'click' with the questions at first, give yourself a break and come back to them at a different time. As I said earlier, people's intuition can work best depending on the time of day and all sorts of other factors, so give yourself time and space to try things out properly.

Caring For Your Intuition

Your intuition is fragile, which is why many people keep it hidden deep inside them where it can't get damaged. As you begin allowing it to surface, it's important to remember that you need to give yourself lots of love and care in order to keep your intuition in good shape. I like to give myself a weekly treat, some relaxing and self-indulgent activity that allows me to recuperate and really makes me feel loved and cared for. I suggest you do the same thing – perhaps book a weekly horse-riding trip, meditation session, cinema visit or spa treatment. Tell your intuition regularly that you care about it and want to look after it.

It's also important to thank your intuition for all the hard work it does for you. When you ask for guidance and receive it, remember to say thank you and feel grateful inside that you've been helped. The more you thank your inner wisdom and feel gratitude in your life, the easier it will be to get in touch with intuitive feelings and you will begin living a life that is rich and supportive and full of answers instead of self-doubt and worry.

When you care for and build a strong bond with your intuition, you unlock a whole new level of higher wisdom that will change your life in many positive and beneficial ways. You are aligning with your higher self, the real you, and not only will this make you feel more confident and intelligent, you'll also learn many secrets and wisdoms of the universe. Once you learn to understand your intuition and your psychic self, you'll find your romantic life moves forward in remarkable ways and you'll feel happier and more in control of your relationships.

Boosting Your Powers of Attraction

I'm now going to show you how to use psychic energy to boost your powers of attraction and draw the right people to you. Many clients contact me because they want to know how to attract the right partner, or they feel they've attracted the wrong partners in the past and don't want to make the same mistake again. When I show them how to improve their psychic attraction energy, I have the pleasure of seeing their romantic lives revitalized as the positive feelings start to flow. On several occasions, I've seen clients go from having no dates and a string of terrible relationships to a choice of three or more wonderful potential partners to share their lives with.

So what's the secret of attraction? Generating the right psychic energy. Whether you realize it or not, life is all about energy. We give out psychic energy and the quality of this energy affects the people around us. Likewise, the energy of those around us can have a large impact on our feelings and behaviour.

Psychic energy is amazing because even those of us

without any spiritual training can sense it in others very easily. When you buy something at the supermarket, you can sense the energy of the cashier even though no words have been exchanged. You can sense whether total strangers are feeling happy, angry, thoughtful or uplifted, and you've probably never really thought all that much about this ability before. But it's amazing, don't you think? After all, no one taught you how to do it and yet you can *feel* whether someone is feeling happy or miserable without them saying a word.

If you were wondering what the difference is between the psychic energy you project to others and the psychic energy you tap into to read other people, there is really very little difference. The energy you give out is what I and other psychic professionals use to read what's going on in your life, and that same energy will attract or repel the people around you depending on what sort of charge it has – negative or positive.

What sort of psychic energy are you giving out? Most of us have friends who leave us feeling drained after just a few hours with them, and equally there are people who lift us up and make us feel great. This is no accident. These people are sending out their own brand of psychic energy and it is attracting or repelling us accordingly. By and large, if you send out positive energy you will attract positive people, and negative energy will attract negative people. There are all sorts of different negative energies when it comes to relationships – aggression, jealousy, insecurity, indifference, sadness and so on – and these will tend to attract like-minded people.

What I want to do is make sure you're generating positive psychic energy so you can attract positive people and situations into your life. First, let's test your psychic energy. What sort of energy are you currently giving out?

Test Your Psychic Energy

Q1. Which of the following words describes you best?

A · Hopeful

B · Realistic

Q2. Which of the following do you think is most important?

A · Mercy

B · Justice

Q3. In your romantic life, would you prefer to:

A · Go on lots of dates and risk being hurt?

B · Only date once in a while but know you're less likely to be rejected?

Q4. Which sentence describes you best?

A · I give easily to others, even strangers.

B · I wait until people earn my trust before I give to them.

Q5. Of the two, would you prefer to:

A · Travel and explore?

B · Create a cosy place to live?

Mostly As: You're sending out mainly positive psychic energy, which will help you attract the right people into your life. But there's no harm in charging up your positive energy, so read the rest of this chapter to discover how to make your psychic energy even more positive and attractive.

Mostly Bs: You're sending out mainly negative energy, so you could be attracting the wrong people, or perhaps no one at all. But don't worry. By the time you've read this chapter, you'll be well on your way to positively charging your psychic energy and bringing great people and romantic situations into your life.

Creating the Energy of Attraction

So how can you ensure your psychic energy is as attractive as possible? I believe the answer lies in your self-esteem.

The number-one thing I've noticed about psychic energy during my years of counselling others is that it is hugely affected by self-esteem. People with low self-esteem have low, negative energy and tend to attract either no one or the wrong types of people, and those who have high self-esteem often have a lot of positive people in their lives. This doesn't always mean they pick the right partners, but having positive people around is certainly a great start!

Even if you usually have high self-esteem, we all have moments when we're feeling low. Perhaps a relationship has just ended or you've lost your job unexpectedly. When you're giving out low psychic energy, this is unfortunately when you attract the wrong people – often at exactly the time you need the love and support of the right people, I'm afraid!

I regularly work with clients to ensure the energy they create around them is in great condition, even if I feel they basically have a good level of self-esteem, as I truly believe giving out positive psychic energy works wonders when it comes to relationships. For all my clients, I recommend this basic exercise to get positive energy flowing:

Powering Up Your Energy of Attraction

I'd like you to set an easy and enjoyable goal for yourself. This could be attending a yoga session if you've never tried yoga before, taking a new evening craft class, taking a long walk in the woods and collecting flowers, making a cake or really anything that makes you feel good whilst you're doing it, and worthwhile once you've finished. I don't want this goal to be anything difficult or time-consuming like learning a new language or teaching yourself how to type – keep it simple and fun please! The goal must also be something you can complete this week, and I'd like you to make arrangements to do just that. If you can complete the goal by the end of the day, even better.

Once you've carried out this goal, you'll feel a rush of positive energy. OK, so if you've been a bit blue of late, perhaps it'll be more like a gentle wave than a rush, but you'll experience some positive feelings nonetheless. I'd like you to really *feel* this happy energy. Where do you experience it in your body and how has your body language changed? By consciously experiencing yourself in a positive energy state, you're building up a template for highly attractive psychic energy. The more you experience positive energy and recognize it, the stronger the template will be. So get practising. With enough practice, you'll be able to call on this template when you want to be attractive to others, and eventually you'll start slotting into this positive energy template all the time.

How Friends Affect Your Psychic Energy

Have you ever been to a music concert and felt uplifted, or attended a wedding and felt loving and peaceful? That's the power of group energy. When a group of people get together, their collective psychic energy is magnified into a powerful force that really can make big changes to the mood of everyone around.

No matter how strong your own psychic energy is, you're influenced by the people around you. Which is why it's very important to surround yourself with positive, supportive people who understand you, your romantic goals and your personality.

How Barbara Boosted Her Psychic Energy

Barbara came to me having recently separated from her husband. A hugely negative man, Barbara's husband had worked for twenty years in a job he hated and saw life as very much toil and struggle. His male friends and their partners were similar – heavy-drinking, complaining, negative people who delighted in other people's misfortune.

After ten years with this man, Barbara's psychic energy was at an all-time low. She was projecting a low mood to all those around her and as a result

---

people often avoided talking to her. She was sure she'd never find another man since she was now 'past her sell-by date' and 'unattractive'. But Barbara hadn't entered her marriage in such a negative state of mind. She told me about her sunshine-filled wedding day and the fun she'd had dating when she was younger. The more we talked, the more I realized she was naturally a very optimistic person whose self-esteem had been sapped by her miserable husband and his friends.

Years of being surrounded by negative energy had a toxic effect on Barbara. Like someone inhaling second-hand cigarette smoke, she was breathing in all her husband's negativity but the process had been so gradual she hadn't noticed that she'd taken that negative energy inside herself.

I encouraged her to get in touch with old friends – people she knew from the days before she met her husband, but only those who were cheerful and had a positive effect on her mood. She found a group of old classmates on 'Friends Reunited' and as she began receiving emails from these forgotten friends she felt her energy lift. This was just the boost she needed to get her psychic energy on the right track, and she was soon feeling much better about herself and sending out a much more attractive energy to others.

When Barbara's ex-husband saw the difference in

his ex-wife, he began pursuing her again, even though he'd ended the marriage to be with another woman. But by then she was wise to him and knew she didn't want to go back to a life of negativity.

Are there people around you who bring you down? People who complain all the time and feed on negative emotions, always looking for the next tragedy or bit of bad news? Negative people leave us feeling exhausted and in a negative frame of mind, and this in turn affects our feelings and self-esteem. The end result? Our psychic energy doesn't attract others.

If you want to send out positive energy and attract the right partner, it's vital you cut out the people in your life who make you feel bad and drain you of positive feelings. But it's not always easy to know who is having a negative effect on you, especially if you're in a downbeat frame of mind yourself. So we're going to use your psychic powers to tune in and seek out the people who are a bad influence on your self-esteem and energy.

Write a list of the five people you see most often in your life. They don't have to be people you're emotionally close to, but simply the people you encounter most regularly. Find a quiet space and look at each name in turn, imagining the person as you do so. What feelings do you get from each name? Allow any images to come too, and note any changes in temperature or your mood.

Now ask your intuition:

Who on this list isn't good for me?

Don't try to pull names into your head. Instead let your intuition whisper the names of people who aren't serving your best needs. It could be these people are perfectly nice and decent, but at this moment in time your lifestyles and habits aren't in sync and this leads to negative conflict that doesn't boost your mood.

If your intuition whispered a few names to you, I want you to think about the steps you're going to take to limit your contact with these people. You don't have to reject them outright or tell them you're cutting them out – after all, they probably need help with their self-esteem too. You can't help anyone unless you're feeling great, so work out the steps you're going to take to keep negative people from using up your time.

I also want you to ask your intuition how to bring new, positive people into your life. Again, find a quiet space, close your eyes if you prefer and ask your higher self:

How can I bring positive people to me?

Don't prejudge the answers that come – they may surprise you, but I promise they will offer very useful guidance.

The Voice of Your Psychic Self

Remember I told you at the beginning of the book that everyone is psychic? Well, guess what – that means others can read you, just as you can read them. What can they read? Your psychic or higher self – the side of you that communicates without you saying a word. The trouble is that when you're feeling down or going through pain, you often lose touch with your higher self and instead a rather negative and unpleasant voice replaces our intuitive wisdom. Some people have perfectly lovely 'out loud' voices and speak kindly to others, but their inner wisdom, the voice that secretly communicates with others, has been replaced by a fake inner voice that is harsh and cruel.

Clients who get in touch with me have sometimes lost touch with their true selves, often because of painful romantic experiences or because they're surrounded by negative people. These are some of the things clients have told me their inner voice tells them on a daily basis:

- I'll never get another relationship
- I'm lonely and unwanted
- I'm lost in limbo and don't know what I'm doing with my life
- I get everything wrong

Outwardly, many of these clients are confident go-getters, but their internal voice, the one others can sense, is saying something quite different and this has had a big impact on their attractiveness.

Let me make something clear. Your true psychic self will *never* say anything critical to you. It may ring some alarm bells and it may give you a sharp emotional prod now and then, but it will never criticize you because its job is to love and protect you. So if your inner voice is saying cruel or demoralizing things, you need to find your true psychic self, and fast.

It's particularly important that when you're dating you

project your true inner voice, the voice of your psychic self that is kind, nurturing, reassuring and forgiving, as this is the voice that will ultimately attract others to you. Believe me, no matter what you're saying out loud, your date will sense any cruel or unkind inner voice whispering unpleasant things inside your head. And this will ring their alarm bells and have them heading towards the door.

Finding Your True Psychic Voice

We're now going to practise using your true psychic voice, the higher wisdom that protects you and always has your best interests at heart. To do this we're going to use an old trick many psychics employ to boost their energy. It is simply positive affirmations. There's no quicker way to find your psychic self than to start using a 'psychic self voice' out loud. But you have to practise often, at least ten times a day, for your inner voice to start matching your outer voice. I would like you to whisper the following things to yourself ten times a day:

- I love myself and will keep myself safe.

- I have unlimited love to give you.

- I am loving and positive and attractive to others.

  Learn these phrases off by heart right now so you can carry them with you throughout the day. Say them whenever you have the urge, but they can be particularly powerful if someone says something negative to you or a situation hasn't gone the way you planned it.

I've recommended positive affirmations to many clients and seen amazing transformations in their romantic and social lives. Love affirmations are simple, but you'll be blown away by how powerful they can be in putting you in touch with your true, loving, psychic voice. Before long you'll start hearing other positive things inside your head – messages, prayers and re-assurances you'll feel really good about hearing. That's when you know your psychic self is talking to you and you're generating a powerful energy of attraction.

Supercharging Your Attractiveness

Now I'd like to really supercharge your attractiveness to make you a magnet for romantic encounters and perfect partners. Those of you who don't like change, be warned – supercharging requires a bold step forward in your life. You are going to shake things up and make big changes and this can be uncomfortable. It can be frightening. But ultimately it will boost your positive energy and your powers of attraction to sky-high levels.

I need you to be completely honest with me. Something in your life isn't working right now and it's draining your psychic energy. Right? Perhaps you're thinking, 'I know what's not working – I don't have a relationship!'

but not being in a relationship is a symptom of low psychic energy, not a cause. What isn't working for you right now? I'm talking something major – job, health, home or relationship. What needs to change in your life to make you feel upbeat and excited and really get your psychic energy flowing?

When I'm working with clients, the same energy drainers come up again and again. What is your energy drainer?

The Top Five Psychic Energy Drainers

Here are the five most common causes of low psychic energy:

- Doing a job that doesn't fit your personality.

- Never really leaving a past relationship behind.

- Being overweight.

- Indulging in a bad habit – smoking, drinking, prescription medication, etc.

- Living in a home or location you don't like.

So now the scary part. You're going to do something about that big something that is draining your psychic energy. Many of my clients live with an energy drainer for a long time, and know deep down they should do something about it. But with their positive psychic self hidden away under pain and fear, they let their false self talk to them. Your false self will tell you all sorts of reasons why you can't change something. You can't start that university course because it's too expensive and there's no way you could ever find the money. You can't totally close the door on your ex because what if you never find anyone else? You can't leave your job because there's no other work out there anyway. Negative thoughts like these come from your false self, not your psychic self.

It's time to listen to your intuition and learn how you're going to get rid of the energy drainer that's suppressing your powers of attraction. In order to do this I'd like you to take yourself somewhere totally new – a place you've never been before. It should be a calm, peaceful place like a park or church, and somewhere you can be alone. Whisper your affirmations to yourself. Relax. Listen to the sounds around you. Smile. Now ask your intuition:

What are the steps I need to take to make this big change in my life?

Your intuition will almost certainly have a few things to tell you right away, but be aware it will also whisper wonderful, inspiring things to you in the days and weeks that follow. Listen and be brave. When you make that big change you'll be astounded at how everything in your life begins to change for the better.

Living with an energy drainer is like lying on a sunny beach in a big coat. No matter how wonderful things are around you, you'll feel tired and uncomfortable and won't really want to make much of an effort. When your energy drainer is removed, your positive psychic energy will soar and not only will you attract happy, loving people into your life, you'll also supercharge your intuition and your psychic abilities.

PART II

The Psychic Secrets of Your Past

6

Understanding Your Past Love Cycles Through Clairvoyance

Do you understand why your past relationships ended? When relationships end, it's rarely a pleasant experience. If a partner has left you, it can devastate your self-esteem and many people find it difficult to move on and start dating again. Equally, I talk with men and women who took the initiative and split with their partner, but were treated badly during the relationship and find it hard to let go of anger and resentment. Perhaps you don't feel devastated or heartbroken, but still wonder why your relationships haven't worked out so far.

Whether you've done the splitting up, or your partner has split with you, the insecurities and self-doubts are often the same. Is there something wrong with me? Why do these bad relationships keep happening? Will I ever find the right partner? It's easy to see a failed relationship as a personal failure, especially if you don't understand where it all went wrong. And if, like many of my clients, you've experienced negative relationship patterns occurring over and over again, it can be even more difficult not to take things personally. Often, people think: 'Why me?

What did I do to deserve all this pain?' Feeling angry and bitter towards an ex is also common, and many individuals fall into a deep depression after a relationship has ended, and feel utterly afraid of making a new commitment in case they're hurt again.

> *If you were hurt in a past relationship, don't worry*
> *– you're not alone.*

Finding someone new is much more difficult if you don't understand the love cycles you've gone through in the past when you've entered dating situations or relationships. If you were hurt in your last relationship, don't worry – you're not alone. I talk to people every day who feel very hurt and betrayed by a past love. It's healthy to go through a period of sadness, anger and 'alone' time when a relationship ends, but if you're angry with your ex-partner, or confused about what went wrong many months after a relationship has ended, the chances are you're holding on to negative energy that is affecting your love life right now. And that negative energy can power you into bad love cycles that go round again and again. What I'd like to do is get you tuning into your intuition and learning from the past so you can break bad love cycles.

You may not even realize you're hanging on to negative emotions, but if you still think about an ex-partner in a way that makes you unhappy or confused, it's more than likely you are. In order to enjoy dating and find true love, you must leave behind all negative energy and break patterns from the past. You do this by learning from the past. Together we're going to look at some of the love cycles people commonly follow, and in the next chapter we're going to use your intuition to answer specific relationship questions I'm often asked.

Why the Truth Hurts – But Also Helps

Now here's an interesting thing. We're often told love is complicated, and that there are all sorts of reasons for relationships breaking down. But during my many years of psychic counselling I've seen the same love cycles repeated again and again. Love isn't complicated. When relationships don't work out, it's because we're living out a bad relationship pattern guaranteed to cause heartache. And if we don't know the truth behind our relationship breakdowns, love can feel very confusing indeed. No wonder people agonize over the 'whys' of past relationships – without truly seeing the love cycle they are stuck in, it's very difficult to avoid the same bad relationship patterns in the future.

Once we find out the real reasons behind a relationship breakdown, it's much easier to avoid the same mistakes in the future.

I've counselled many clients who've lived out the same bad relationship over and over again. Their partners change, but the relationship is basically the same. They're reliving the same negative relationship cycle, like a hamster stuck in a wheel. To break the cycle, you need to understand your common dating mistakes, ask the right questions and let go of all your hurt, confusion and negative energy.

Deep down, most people know this. That's why I receive thousands of phone calls from men and women desperate to discover why a relationship ended. We all know that once we find the reasons behind a break-up we can avoid the same mistakes in the future. When we talk endlessly with friends about a past relationship, or seek advice from a psychic counsellor, or obsess about an ex in our minds, we're really trying to find the truth that will prevent future heartache. This is very healthy. The trouble is, without an awareness of our psychic abilities we doubt ourselves. We dream up lots of different 'truths' and we're not sure which is the right one. When you tune into your psychic powers, you'll *know* the bad cycles you keep going through. You'll understand your past and be well on your way to breaking negative relationship patterns and finding true love.

However, a word of warning: discovering the truth can be painful. Sometimes it can be shocking. But I promise you, it's much less painful than going through heartache after heartache, never understanding why your relationships don't work and constantly doubting yourself. The truth will set you free from hurt, and put you on the path to a happy, healthy relationship.

Using Your Psychic Powers to Discover Your Love Cycles

So how are you going to find the truth about your past love cycles? Well, actually, you won't be 'finding' it at all, because you already know it. The answers are inside you, just waiting to make a connection. If you're not emotionally ready to know the truth, then the answers may just wait a little longer for you to find them. But if you're ready to leave the old patterns behind and meet your true love, then you'll find it very easy to connect with your psychic self and discover the truth you're looking for.

When you discover the truth about your relationship patterns, you'll feel a tremendous sense of relief. Not only will you be able to let go of any anger or bad feelings towards your ex-lovers, you'll feel more secure and happy. No longer will you doubt yourself or question your ability to find true love. You'll feel like a heavy cage of blame, anger and confusion has been lifted, and you'll be free to explore love in healthier, happier ways.

So let's discover more about your past love cycles and help you move on and find happiness. Here are the five negative love cycles I see clients repeat over and over again:

You Never Get Past the First Few Dates

Some people can never seem to get past the first few dates and into a committed relationship. It's as though there's an invisible block that stops them getting serious. Either their date loses interest, or they do, but no matter what, a relationship never seems to get going.

He Leaves You For His Ex

Many of my clients attract love on the rebound. That's to say, they're free and single but the person they attract is still secretly holding a candle for his ex and eventually ends up returning to his past relationship.

He Stops Calling You

I've often counselled people whose dates or relationships are hot one day, cold the next. Whenever they date someone, it starts out amazingly and they think true love is on the cards. And then bang! One day the passion vanishes and they're left hurt and confused.

He Cheats on You

A particularly painful cycle. For some, it seems their date or partner can never commit to just one person. The people they see are always unfaithful, and there are usually lots of lies and secretive behaviour that come as part of this love cycle too.

He's Not Good Enough For You

On paper it looks good, but the relationship just doesn't feel quite right. Not exciting enough, not enough chemistry, not enough things in common . . . the list goes on. So inevitably it always ends as you're forever looking over your shoulder for something better.

Do any of these cycles sound familiar? I'm now going to ask you to use your intuition to discover which love cycles connect to you. You may instantly feel drawn to one or two of the cycles, but I want to make sure that logic isn't getting in the way. Sometimes, we think we know ourselves, but the truth is quite different. You may think you're always attracted to people who cheat, but the truth is you always go for people who are on the rebound and return to their exes, for example. So I'd like you to draw a little picture of each love cycle on pink paper. The picture can be of whatever you like, but you have to know what it represents. Don't write any words. Then I want you to go somewhere calm, breathe slowly and wait for your intuition to guide you towards the picture that best represents your past cycle.

Even if you don't understand why you're drawn towards a particular picture, don't discount it. We're getting in touch with your hidden powers here, your secret intuition that isn't always logical but is always right.

What is your major negative love cycle? Perhaps you've been stuck in more than one negative cycle in the past. But by talking to your intuition, you've just unlocked the major tool that will help you break free.

Psychic Alarm Bells

I'm now going to help you get an even clearer picture of your past relationships, and help you learn a valuable tool for avoiding bad love cycles. What is this tool? Your psychic ability to hear 'psychic alarm bells'. What are psychic alarm bells? They're your intuition trying to tell you something and they ring during all bad relationships – even when the relationships seem to be going well. They don't always ring very loudly (if only they did), and if you don't tune into your psychic energy they're often very hard to hear. But they're always there, ringing away, if something isn't right. Have you ever replayed a situation in your head after a relationship has ended, and said to yourself: *I knew something wasn't right when he said that, or did this . . .*? That's a psychic alarm bell, and you're going to learn how to use those bells to help you pinpoint what went wrong in your relationships.

We're going to take a quick look at your last two relationships or dating experiences and see if we can identify the alarm bells that should have stopped you taking love any further. So let's talk about your story, and help you get psychic. I want you to take a pen and some lined paper, find a quiet space and write out three or four pages about your last two relationships or dates, from how you met and got together to how it all ended. You won't have to show this to anyone, and as soon as we've worked on your story together you can chuck the paper in the bin. I really want you to get in touch with your intuition whilst you're writing. Feel as calm as you can and let the words flow. Don't think too much. And try to remember feelings about things, rather than words that were said.

Did he ever talk about his ex-girlfriend and, if so, how did you feel at the time? Were there any unexplained date cancellations, text messages or bad moods? What were the situations that gave you cause for alarm, but you brushed over because you wanted everything to work out? Did you just *feel* like there were times he was cooling off?

Remember your psychic alarm bells, and know they give you the power to break free from the past and find true love.

OK. Now I'd like you to take a good look at what you've written and tell me which warning signs you chose to ignore during your dates and relationship. If you can't see any, just give yourself a little more time and the answers should come. If you really, really can't spot any psychic alarm bells, then it's back to the drawing board: get writing again and see what other memories come to the surface.

I guarantee that during this experience you'll spot at least one psychic alarm bell, and most likely four or five. Now here is the important part. Learn from them! Once you are aware of your psychic alarm bells, you own the key to freedom from the reoccurring love cycles that keep you trapped in bad relationships. What were the signs you chose to ignore? Moodiness? Ex-girlfriends on the scene? Disinterest? Not returning your calls? Flirting with your friends? Yes, I know these alarm bells can hurt – that's why you should have listened to them sooner. Your psychic self sent them to protect you.

You will feel most strongly about the warning signs that teach you the most important lessons and warn you loudly about your negative love cycles. That is your intuition at work. You may feel frightened, angry, sad or hopeless when you think of these warning bells. These feelings are love lessons and they will pass in time. But for now they are the keys to your freedom. Keep the keys close, and feel happy that you now have the power to break free from the past and move forward.

In the next chapter, we'll look at specific answers to questions about past relationships so you can find out in more detail just why you attract certain love cycles and how to break free.

7

Finding the Answers to Painful Questions

Now your psychic self has taught you more about your negative love cycles, how are you feeling? A little fragile and vulnerable? Maybe even angry? The truth can be painful, so give yourself permission to work through any bad feelings. By the time you've finished this book you'll be feeling much better, I absolutely promise you. Sometimes it takes a while to digest the truth and let it become a part of you. Perhaps your broken heart won't be a hundred per cent mended straight away, but over time I guarantee it will be, and you'll feel totally confident that you'll find true love, be happy and put the past behind you.

Are you ready to find the answers you've been waiting for, and move on with your life? In this chapter, we'll ask the five major love questions I'm often asked when I talk to clients. They each relate to a negative love cycle, so by asking the question and hearing the answer you will move even closer to freeing yourself from the negative patterns of the past.

I'm going to share with you the painful relationship questions I hear every day.

When I work with clients, we use my intuition to learn the answers to their questions. I do this by working with the knowledge I already have with thousands of my client relationships, and then plugging into my intuition and letting the answers to a specific client's situation come to me.

This is what I'm going to show you how to do. I'm going to share with you the major relationship questions I hear every day, and the experiences of clients I've helped to answer those questions. By listening to negative relationship experiences, you'll learn to spot the bad relationship patterns that reoccur in all failed relationships. In Chapter 8, we'll tune into your psychic powers and learn the answers that relate to your specific past dates and relationships.

If you wish, you can choose to read only the chapters that ask the questions you'd like answered, but I'd recommend reading all the chapters in this section. You may discover answers to questions you didn't even know needed answering.

Heartbreak Question 1: Why Can I Never Get Past the First Date?

It's very common for clients to call me because they've been on lots of first dates, but never seem to make it to date number two. For whatever reason, they just don't click with their date and they never receive that second call that signals the possible beginning of a relationship.

In fact, being 'dumped' after the first date is so common that I've spoken to many women who think perhaps it would just be easier to be single than suffer the humiliation of dating and not being asked out again.

So I'm going to share with you the reasons why, in my experience, people don't get asked out again after a first date and hopefully put some of your worries and anxieties to rest and help you reach that magical second date.

Rhea's Twenty-Six First Dates

When Rhea came to see me, she'd been on *twenty-six* first dates but had never been asked on a second. She was beginning to think something was wrong with her and was thinking about giving up dating altogether to spare herself the pain of rejection. True, a few of those dates she had rejected herself, but the majority had simply never invited her out a second time.

Rhea was a very sexy, sassy lady who liked going out clubbing and generally met men late at night in bars and clubs. She was curvy and glamorous and adored making herself look great for a big night out. Invariably someone would flirt with her, ask for her number and call the next day to arrange a date.

> **When I tuned into Rhea's energy, I got a strong sense of mismatch.**

However, the Rhea who met men in clubs was different from the Rhea who went on dates. When she dated, she wore jeans and an altogether more casual look as she was, in her words, 'Looking for a serious relationship, not just sex.'

Rhea told me she often noticed her date's face drop when she met him in the 'cold light of day', and this reaction was beginning to have a negative affect on her confidence. The date would usually progress well enough, but afterwards there would be no affection or interest from the man and then he simply wouldn't call again. Often, Rhea would ask towards the end of the date, 'So, how about doing this again?' but this would be met with a non-committal response.

When I tuned into Rhea's energy, I got a strong sense of mismatch with the men she went on dates with. They wanted something casual, whereas she was after something long term.

I explained to Rhea that, in my experience, when men are out in nightclubs they are often looking for sexual conquests rather than serious relationships. By 'winning' her phone number, they were enjoying what they felt to be a conquest, but a full-blown relationship with Rhea wasn't really what they wanted.

When Rhea turned up on a date in casual clothes, Rhea's dates realized that she was more interested in a serious relationship than sex and this made them feel pressured – particularly when she suggested a second date. They didn't want to lead her on or hurt her feelings, so they simply didn't ask her out again.

Psychic Alarm Bells

What are the psychic alarm bells that suggest you're dating a man who won't ask you out again?

- You asked him out and arranged the date.

- You met whilst both of you were drunk.

- He doesn't try to impress you or offer to pay the bill.

- The date ends ahead of schedule.

- He doesn't make sure you get home safely.

- He doesn't compliment you during the date.

Why Don't Men Ask Women Out on Second Dates?

I often find women aren't asked out on second dates because they're dating the wrong men. Perhaps the men they meet are only looking for a casual fling and get cold feet at the thought of commitment. Or perhaps they just have very little in common with the woman they're dating. Sometimes men enjoy the 'thrill of the chase', but once they've caught their prize the thrill is over and they need another woman to run after. Obviously this is not the sort of man you want to be dating if you're looking for a serious relationship.

Rhea's story is a typical one in that she was meeting

men in all the wrong places. She wanted a long-term relationship but she met men in places where sex was at the top of the agenda. Once these men met her in her casual clothes, the promise of sex was a long way off and they immediately lost interest.

If you never seem to get past the first date, take a good look at where you're meeting your potential love interests because they obviously don't match you or your needs. Perhaps the people you meet aren't interested in long-term commitment, or perhaps they simply don't share your interests and lifestyle.

Think seriously about the type of person you want to meet and ask your intuition for help. Don't date just anyone – be particular. Make sure there is a good chance you and your date are compatible and that they are single and looking for a long-term relationship *before* you go out with them. Also, take a look at Chapter 9, which will tell you all about Internet dating and how to find the right websites to meet people serious about long-term commitment.

Do you feel like these are the right answers for you? If you're not sure, I'd advise you to read the other 'Heartbreak Questions' in this chapter too to see if there are other answers that fit better. You *know* the answers, because you're psychic. They may be painful at first, but in your heart you know the truth. And once you know, I promise the pain will ease. You'll stop feeling like you're going crazy, wondering, 'Why, why, why?' all the time, and be ready to move on with your life.

Heartbreak Question 2: Why Did He Leave Me for His Ex?

Being dumped for an ex is horrible. Nobody likes to feel they were only ever the understudy in a relationship, whilst the real star of the show was waiting in the wings all along. I've counselled women whose husbands or long-term partners have run off with a former lover, but it's much more common for people to be thrown aside for the 'dreaded ex' in the early stages of dating. Why? You'll find out shortly. However it happens, I know it hurts to have a relationship end this way. A lot. Whenever I'm contacted by a client who has been abandoned for an old flame, I know their self-esteem is likely to be in tatters and they need an extra helping of TLC.

The good news is that, in this situation, the answers really can bring instant relief. If you don't know why your man left you for his ex, it's easy to imagine all sorts of terrible reasons that are damaging to your self-esteem. *Am I not pretty enough? Am I not girlfriend material? Did he leave because my middle toes are longer than my big toes?* When you discover the real reasons why many men go back to their former partners, you'll realize it has very little to do with you at all – except for the fact that you chose him to have a relationship with. You will learn how to spot the men who are likely to run off with their former loves, to leave them well alone and only date available men who are ready for a relationship with you.

*I'll take you through the psychic intuition process to
discover exactly what went wrong.*

If your date or partner has dropped you for their former
lover, I promise you're not alone. Hundreds of men and
women contact me, desperate to know why their partner
ran off with the 'dreaded ex' and I take them through the
psychic intuition process of discovering exactly why everything went wrong, just as I will do for you. Believe me,
you're not the only one who has been in this situation, and
you will get over it and move on. Not only that, but by tapping into your psychic abilities you'll make sure you'll never
make the same mistake in the future.

Angela's Love Triangle

I'm going to share with you now the story of Angela, who
was dumped by her date for his ex-girlfriend. The details
of Angela's story may be different from yours, but I'm
certain there will be similarities – and I'd like you to try
and spot these as you read about her experience.

Angela called me several years ago in a state of real
confusion and despair. She'd been seeing a man called
Simon who had left her without giving any reason what-
soever, and she was absolutely desperate to find out why.

We spoke a little about how the two of them met, their
personalities and how the dating had gone so far. Appar-
ently, when Angela first met Simon, he was very keen
indeed, even mentioning further commitment – which
was a little overwhelming for Angela. They began to see

each other about twice a week, with regular contact in between dates, and Angela grew to see Simon as great relationship potential. They'd go out to dinner together, then on to a pub or bar, but they always visited venues Simon had never been to before. He never took Angela to any of his old haunts. Within a few weeks Simon began to stay over at Angela's place. She started opening up to him, sharing intimate details about her life, cooking him meals and ringing him to talk about her day.

> *If someone you're seeing ditches you for their ex, it feels like the rug has been well and truly pulled from under you.*

After a month and a half, Simon abruptly stopped calling and didn't answer any of Angela's calls or text messages. It was very hurtful for Angela to be totally ignored by a man who, up until recently, she'd been very intimate with, not to mention embarrassing to have no response to her calls. She felt absolutely desperate to find out what was going on, and had a stream of questions for me: *Was it me? What did I do wrong? Is he seeing someone else?* Suddenly, Angela had no clue what was happening in her life.

During our counselling session, I had a strong feeling that someone else was involved – a lady who had been on the scene before Angela and Simon started dating. When I mentioned this idea to Angela, she remembered that Simon had still been in contact with an ex-girlfriend when they started dating, but he told her the relationship was finished – albeit very recently. We talked about this, and I grew certain this ex-girlfriend was the cause of Simon's unexplained departure.

> *It's not uncommon for men to go back to their ex-girlfriends, but it never has to happen to you ever again.*

Angela and I were in contact over several months, and four months later my suspicions were confirmed: a friend of Angela's discovered that Simon had indeed returned to his ex-girlfriend. Now that Angela knew the reason Simon had left, she really, really wanted to know *why* he'd decided to leave her for his ex. The familiar low self-esteem questions reared their ugly heads: *Is she more attractive than me? Did I do something wrong that put him off? Will I ever find anyone who is over their ex?*

I explained to Angela that, sadly, it's not uncommon for some men to go back to ex-girlfriends. It seemed clear to me by Simon's behaviour that he was very much on the rebound. He'd recently split up with his ex and still talked about her and stayed in touch. And he didn't want to take Angela to any of his old haunts. This suggests there was unresolved emotional pain associated with these places and/or he didn't want to bump into a recent ex-girlfriend with a date as he wanted to keep his options open. The fact that he'd only very recently split with his ex suggested he was either a very callous person or looking to soothe a broken heart by finding love on the rebound.

In my head, I heard two loud bells ringing when Angela told me her story. The first bell was when I learned Simon kept in touch with his ex. Not a crime in itself, but Angela obviously felt uneasy enough to log this in her memory. Bell two: Simon was really keen in the beginning, almost too keen. Men who come on very strong before they know much about you should wear a warning sticker saying, 'Something's not right here!' There were more alarm bells, but these were the major signs to me – mainly because they were the signs that my intuition told me were most important.

Psychic Alarm Bells

What are the psychic alarm bells that suggest a man might leave you for his ex?

- He's only just split up with his girlfriend – perhaps within the last week or month.

- He's still in touch with his ex-girlfriend, but they don't have any children together, mutual friends or shared work commitments.

- He complains about his ex-girlfriend and blames her for the relationship ending.

- He talks a lot about his past relationship, even though you don't ask about it.

- He acts like he's in love with you, but in your heart you know he doesn't know you all that well.

Do any of these sound familiar?

Why Do Men Go Back to Their Exes?

Every relationship is different, but after working with hundreds of clients I tend to find men return to their exes because they were never over them in the first place. It's sad, but many men start a new relationship on the rebound to try and mend their own broken heart. Often, they themselves were dumped and didn't want their past relationship to end, so are more than happy to go running back to their ex at the first opportunity.

In Angela's case, Simon had only split up with his long-term girlfriend a month before he started seeing Angela. Again, this should have sounded a big alarm bell. If a man has been seeing someone for many years, no matter what he tells you (we've been growing apart for a while, it was never serious, and so on) most healthy individuals take a few months to heal and move on.

> *Deep down, you may not think highly enough of yourself to think you deserve a man with a clean slate.*

I've known clients who've been happily married for several years and then out of the blue their husband runs off with his ex-girlfriend. This is devastating and very painful. Feelings of inferiority come thick and fast. But usually the same reason applies. I discover, by having them talk over early dating experiences and channelling my intuition, that the 'rebound factor' is right there and plain for all to see. Worse, my client inevitably knew at the beginning of the relationship that they were stepping into someone else's shoes, but ignored all their intuitive signals and assumed their man would change and in time fall in love with them completely.

Why Do You Attract Men on the Rebound?

Deep down women often don't think highly enough of themselves to feel they deserve a man with a clean slate. I see this time and time again with my clients. They ignore the signs that a man isn't over his ex because deep down they don't think they're worthy of a healthy, kind man who values them exclusively. On the surface they might say, 'I thought he would change,' but inside they really think, 'I just wanted somebody, anybody, and he seemed to like me well enough.' By using Chapter 5 to boost your self-esteem and your powers of attraction, you'll help overcome deep-rooted bad feelings about yourself and break free of rebound relationships.

So just to clarify: it's not you, it's him. Let's say that again: it's *really* not you, and it *really* is him. His ex is no better than you are, she's no more attractive or sweet or lovely, you haven't done anything wrong and you're certainly great relationship material.

Your only crime is to have picked the wrong man and not thought highly enough of yourself to think you deserve someone without an ex lurking in the background. When you're not connecting with your psychic energy or your powers of attraction, these mistakes are very easy to make. You deserve better than a man on the rebound, and together we're going to find it for you.

Heartbreak Question 3: Why Did He Stop Calling?

When you're dating, it's very confusing and hurtful to suddenly be given the cold shoulder – especially if you thought things were going well. Clients often contact me after a first date, wondering why their romantic match hasn't called, or perhaps they've been on several dates and been confused and upset to find the phone line has gone dead. Either way, they want answers, and we work together using both my psychic senses and my years of love counselling experience to discover what's going on.

When Samantha's Date Stopped Calling

Let me tell you about a client of mine called Samantha. She started dating a man in his late thirties (she was thirty-one at the time) called Harry, whom she'd met through mutual friends.

Harry was very much an alpha male, insisting on opening doors for Samantha and picking her up in his car for their dates, and sometimes Samantha found herself playing down her own intelligence for fear it might 'put him off'. Harry was also very flash with his cash, taking Samantha to places she'd never ordinarily have chosen, but she was happy to have new experiences. Harry took Samantha on several dates, including a boat trip along the Thames, and as they spent more time together Samantha assumed their relationship was growing more serious.

But as their dates progressed, Samantha felt that Harry

was becoming colder and more distant. Whereas at first he'd rung her regularly and always returned her calls, now he frequently didn't ring for weeks at a time and if she rang him he took days to ring her back. She assumed he was simply entering the 'comfort zone' where he didn't feel he had to make so much of an effort, and Samantha convinced herself that this was probably a good thing.

On their last date, which had been cancelled and re-arranged by Harry several times, Samantha asked him where the relationship was going. Harry said he wasn't sure, but hoped they could continue having fun together.

After that, Harry stopped calling and didn't return any of Samantha's answer-machine messages. She was humiliated and resorted to bombarding him with text messages, but still there was no reply. Samantha was left embarrassed and confused, sorely regretting all the messages she'd sent but still desperately wanting an answer as to why Harry had ended all contact.

Psychic Alarm Bells

What are the psychic alarm bells that suggest a man might stop calling you?

- You sense him withdrawing during your time together.

- He never makes any firm time commitments.

- He's very late for dates or reschedules without good reason.

- You just *know* he's not as interested as he was at first – perhaps he's stopped paying for your meals or opening doors for you, or you just have a feeling.

- He waits a long time before calling you, and if you call him he waits days before returning your call.

Why Do Men Stop Calling?

In my experience, men stop calling because they don't think a relationship will work in the long term. This is a truth I've seen time and time again and yes – the truth can be painful. For many of us, dating comes at a challenging time in our lives when we're not feeling at our best and need as much love and acceptance as possible. It's tough to know that someone you dated doesn't want to be with you long term and hasn't even had the decency to let you know face-to-face.

But let's put things into perspective. If your date doesn't see a long-term future with you, this *doesn't* mean you're unattractive, unlovable or unappealing. It simple means this: the two of you aren't right together, and *he* worked it out before you did.

Maybe you simply weren't compatible as a couple, or perhaps your date wasn't emotionally in the right place to commit and wanted to spare you the pain of an 'on again, off again' relationship. Either way, really you should be celebrating. You've escaped a potential bad relationship and are now free and able to find a great one.

I don't want to sound flippant when I talk about 'celebrating' when men stop calling. I know it hurts, and in Samantha's case she really was devastated. But often, we're upset not because we think we've lost 'the one', but because our *hopes* of happiness have been snatched away.

If you're hurt because someone hasn't called you back, remember that happiness really has to come from you.

If you're hurt about someone not returning your call, the correct question to ask your intuition is: *Why weren't we right together?* The true answer isn't hurtful and it won't damage your self-esteem. Better still, it will point you towards the right men and the right relationship.

Samantha was sure she felt awful because Harry was the one for her and she'd lost true love. But Samantha was really looking for a relationship to make her happy, rather than building happiness from within. This meant that when Harry stopped calling her, she felt empty, hollow, unhappy and desperate to win him back. Deep down, it wasn't really Harry she was interested in but a relationship – any relationship.

My sense was that Harry was simply too fast-paced and fiery for Samantha, and in a long-term relationship her gentle, emotional side wouldn't have been nurtured. There was nothing wrong with Samantha at all, or Harry for that matter, but the two of them together weren't compatible and Harry realized this.

Samantha confirmed that there were many times during

their dates when Harry would talk over her or make decisions for her, but she didn't listen to these 'alarm bells' as she so badly wanted the happiness a relationship would bring.

If you're hurt because someone hasn't called you back, remember that happiness really has to come from you. Loving yourself is imperative to finding a great relationship and weathering the inevitable knocks that come with dating. When it comes to love, the occasional rejection is part of the journey, but if you work on your own happiness you'll move on much more quickly if the phone stops ringing.

Ask your intuition:
What makes me happy?
What makes me feel good?
What other things, outside of a relationship, do I enjoy?
How can I enjoy my own company?

Work on your own happiness and I promise you'll feel OK if a man doesn't call you back because you'll know this means he's the wrong man. Remember, if it's the right time and you've found the right man, he'll always call.

Heartbreak Question 4: Why Did He Cheat on Me?

'Ouch' is the word that springs to mind when clients tell me their partner cheated on them. Cheating causes emotional pain, but I often find with my clients that the greatest pain comes because deep down they knew their partner wasn't faithful. When a client tells me they've discovered their date is a love cheat, it is rarely a complete surprise. Even if they're shocked at first, images and memories begin to surface and they realize the signs were there all along.

But, of course, clients still want to know *why* their partner cheated. So let's answer that question right now.

Teresa's Roaming Romeo

Teresa contacted me in a state of deep depression and despair. She'd dated thirty-five people in the last year and had just discovered that lucky number thirty-five, the man she'd been seeing for six months, had been seeing two other women besides her. Ouch. Her date, Sebastian, was upset at being caught out and begged for Teresa's forgiveness, but he wasn't at all bothered when she ended their relationship and this is probably what hurt Teresa the most.

When I asked Teresa how she and Sebastian had met, she told me it was at a work networking event. She'd been wearing, in her words, her 'knock-out' outfit and Sebastian had made a beeline for her and taken her out for dinner the very next night.

Teresa had been uncertain about Sebastian at first as he seemed very keen, even though he didn't know her well. But after a few dates Teresa really believed they might have a future together. She'd stayed over at Sebastian's house a few times (despite being warned by work colleagues that he was known as the 'office Romeo'), and really felt she was special to him and the two of them were good together.

What are the psychic alarm bells that suggest you're dating a potential love cheat?

After the first month or so, the initial passion died down and Sebastian stopped calling Teresa so frequently. He'd send a text sometimes to 'check in' as she called it, but it was now down to Teresa to call and arrange dates if she wanted to see Sebastian. This situation frustrated Teresa, but because Sebastian had been so keen in the beginning she felt it was her turn to make the calls.

Sometimes, when Teresa went out with Sebastian, she was surprised at how little he really seemed to know about her, considering they'd been seeing each other for a little while. He often forgot basic details such as where she worked, or her birthday. He was also very particular about his mobile phone and laptop, getting very touchy if she ever asked to use either of them.

Eventually, Teresa received a text from a girl claiming to be Sebastian's girlfriend and asking what Teresa's number was doing on his phone. Sebastian dismissed the text as from his 'crazy ex-girlfriend', but Teresa called the woman and together the pair discovered Sebastian was two-timing them both. Teresa secretly checked Sebastian's phone and found a third woman he was also dating. She was devastated and felt stupid and used.

Psychic Alarm Bells

What are the psychic alarm bells that suggest you're dating a potential love cheat?

- You sometimes feel he's keeping you at arm's length and you don't get to see him as much as you feel is normal in a dating situation.

- There are rumours about other women he is seeing.

- He's dated lots of women, but none of them have a good word to say about him.

- He never talks about commitment, nor indicates that you're in an exclusive relationship.

- He goes AWOL from time to time and is impossible to contact.

Why Did He Cheat on You?

Men cheat for lots of reasons, but I often find that in a dating situation a man 'cheats' because he still sees himself as free and single. How do you know when a man is committed only to you? In my experience, he'll tell you. He'll say he's going to be faithful only to you, and ask for a similar commitment on your side. He may not use those exact words, but one way or another he'll let you know that from now on you're the only woman in his life. Many of us are romantic souls and 'hear' commitment where there isn't any. If a man takes us away for a weekend, we assume this means he's very committed. If he comes and meets our family or tells us he loves spending time with us, we think it must be true love. But if a man hasn't promised commitment, then he may well feel there is no reason why he can't see several women at once.

On the other hand, some men really are just serial cheaters and addicted to the thrill of the chase. It's unlucky to come across this sort of man, but if your intuition is in good shape you'll be warned well in advance and stay away in future.

What signs did he give that suggested long-term commitment?

Was your love cheat really just an ordinary guy who hadn't promised you any special commitment? Or were you unlucky enough to fall for a man addicted to the thrill of the chase? What does your intuition tell you?

It's much more comfortable to believe a love cheat is really a love rat who will treat all women badly, but – truthfully – did your date promise to be faithful to you? What signs did he give that suggested long-term commitment? Were there any, or did your imagination take over?

If your intuition tells you your partner really was simply a serial love rat, you should be very aware that you let this man into your life and made your feelings vulnerable to him. This suggests you weren't properly tuning into your intuitive powers. Ask your intuition:

How can I stay away from these sorts of men in future?

Heartbreak Question 5: Why is No One Ever Good Enough?

Many of my clients contact me because they've been cheated on or treated badly, but it can be just as heartbreaking if you never seem to meet anyone you feel the right connection with. Maybe you're forever going on first dates, only to reject someone almost immediately for not being right. Or perhaps you have a habit of entering longer-term, comfortable relationships, knowing the spark isn't really there and you'll have to break it off eventually. If you're always meeting people who aren't quite right, you might despair at ever finding 'the one'. But worry not. Your intuition and my psychic counselling experience are here to help.

Why Kaitlyn's Dates Were Never Quite Right

When Kaitlyn came to see me, I could tell she was a fiercely independent, strong and clear-minded woman. She'd had a string of dating experiences, but had never seen any one man for more than six months because, for one reason or another, she'd decided her date didn't have long-term potential.

She'd recently been seeing a man called John, but what had at first seemed like a promising relationship had ended after just a few weeks. 'We didn't have any of the same interests,' Kaitlyn explained. Kaitlyn was an excellent horse rider and had encouraged John to come along for a riding lesson with her. Although he tried his best, John wasn't a natural with horses and because of this Kaitlyn decided a long-term match just wouldn't work out. 'How can I think about settling down with someone who doesn't share one of my greatest interests?' she said.

Before John, she'd been seeing a man who worked as a postman. 'He was lovely,' she told me, 'but I needed someone who was more ambitious. Being with a postman just wouldn't have worked long term.'

Deep down, Kaitlyn was scared of emotional pain.

Kaitlyn asked me to do some forecasting and find out if there was a soulmate in her future, as she was really beginning to lose hope. When I psychically analysed her past relationships, it seemed to me she'd been lucky enough to find plenty of lovely men. However, I could sense a lot of pain and fear, so I asked Kaitlyn where this might be coming from.

With much emotion, she confessed that years ago she'd dated a man who'd left her to start a homosexual relationship. Having been uncertain about his sexuality for years, the man had dated Kaitlyn in the hope he could make a male–female relationship work but eventually decided he preferred men.

This had caused much embarrassment and upset for Kaitlyn, and as a result she was ruthless with men, fitting them into a rigid template to try and avoid dating anyone unsuitable. Deep down, Kaitlyn was scared of reliving emotional pain, so she tried to protect herself by ditching men before she really gave them a chance.

It's good to be picky when it comes to love – if only some of my clients were *more* picky. But if you find yourself rejecting men over and over again, my experience tells me you might be scared of the pain that can occur when a relationship doesn't work out.

Psychic Alarm Bells

What are the psychic alarm bells that suggest you're rejecting men because you're scared of emotional commitment?

- You feel uneasy if your date suggests making joint commitments for the future.

- You don't feel attracted to or excited by 'nice guys', or guys who are too keen.

- You wouldn't consider a relationship with someone who has different interests to you.

- You like to be completely in control of when and where you meet for your dates.

- You expect your dates to change to suit your lifestyle.

Why Isn't Anyone Good Enough for You?

If you're always rejecting men, the chances are you're scared of getting hurt. Of course, every situation is different. It is entirely possible that you just haven't met the right man yet, and have so far let psychic alarm bells help you avoid the wrong men – there are a few frogs out there after all. But by and large, in my experience, if you're always dating people and finding fault with them, you're scared of emotional commitment and the possible pain this could involve.

What does your intuition tell you? What do you feel inside to be true? Are you well tuned-in and simply brushing aside the Mr Wrongs, or are you turning away men with real potential because your fear dial is turned way up and you're worried that unless someone meets an exact criteria of perfection they might hurt your feelings?

If you think you might be scared of rejection and emotional commitment, ask your intuition: *What's happened in my past to make me feel this way?* This feeling hasn't come out of nowhere. Has something happened in your family that made you feel abandoned or insecure? Or did a past relationship break your trust and your heart, and deep down you've never really got over this betrayal?

> **When you're in touch with your psychic self you'll know for certain which dates deserve a chance.**

Often, clients who are scared of rejection are confident, happy, successful people who for some reason or another have lost trust in others. They feel they can only trust themselves, and therefore keep tight control on everything, from where they live and work to how their relationships unfold.

But romance isn't like a career path. Your heart has to be open if you're going to find Mr Right, and that means letting go of control and appreciating that you might be in for a bumpy emotional ride whilst looking for your soul-mate.

The good news is that by reading this book and getting in touch with your intuition, you're making great steps towards emotional openness and confidence. When you feel strongly connected with your psychic self, you'll feel much more able to take emotional risks and let your guard down. Rather than let fear control your decisions, you'll be tapping into your higher self – the self that really *knows* who's right for you. It might be Mr Right doesn't share all your interests or be exactly as you expected, but when you're in touch with your psychic self you'll know for certain which dates deserve a chance.

8

Tuning In, Clearing Energy and Moving On

One of the keys to finding love lies in recognizing what went wrong in past relationships and letting go of negative feelings. Once you let go of the past, you can break free of bad relationship patterns, open your heart and welcome new love into your life.

Learning about why relationships commonly end, as we did in the previous chapter, can offer tremendous relief and put burning questions to rest. But I'd also like you to get specific about your own relationship patterns, and really tune into any unique messages your intuition has for you about reoccurring bad relationships.

In this chapter I'll show you a great technique for tuning in, recognizing bad relationship patterns and moving towards the relationship you really want. Then we're going to work on clearing bad emotions. You're going to release any negative energy that has been preventing you from finding a great partner up until now. By the end of this chapter, you'll feel uplifted, full of good feelings and positive about your loving, happy future.

Breaking Out of the Negative Relationship Cycle

You've heard the phrase 'like attracts like' haven't you? It's true. When you experience a bad relationship, you often start thinking about what you *don't* want, rather than what you do want, and as a result your psychic energy sends out the 'don't want' signals and brings you the same bad relationships over and over again.

Often, my clients who are in bad relationship cycles have low self-esteem and just can't picture anything other than a problematic relationship. They know they don't want someone who cheats or is emotionally unavailable but their energy gives out very different signals.

Is there a pattern to your previous relationships? Are you always attracting the wrong sorts of partner? Do any of these negative relationships sound familiar?

- Your partner focuses too much on his career
- Your partner is jealous and aggressive
- Your partner isn't supportive
- Your partner is married, or for some reason unable to commit
- Your partner doesn't make any effort in the relationship
- Your partner cheats on you

I'm always amazed by how often people repeat bad relationships – choosing people who share the same negative characteristics as a previous partner, and sometimes even look and dress the same too. What is your common dating mistake? If the answer doesn't jump into your head immediately, make a list of your past relationships and next to each one list three key things that made you unhappy. Are there any patterns?

If there's a pattern to your past bad relationships, generally this is because you're holding on to some negative feelings and projecting these out, without realizing it, in the psychic aura around you. These bad feelings can come from the past relationships themselves, or from other places such as family or childhood experiences. These are the sorts of negative thoughts people project without realizing it:

I'm so desperate for a relationship, I'll go out with anyone who'll have me.

I don't want another jealous boyfriend.

I don't believe anyone healthy would be interested in me.

I don't want another career-minded boyfriend who has no time for a relationship.

I'm not good enough for anyone.

I don't want another married man.

Negative psychic energy attracts negative relationships, so it's vital to find the positive, higher self inside you and let this be the voice that speaks out. The more you work at seeking out your kind, positive intuition, the more you'll work against the usual relationship patterns and attract kind, positive people. Your higher self wants to bring you a great relationship, so the key is to listen to what you want, *not* what you don't want. Transform all thoughts of what you don't want into something positive, and reverse any self-defeating negative talk. So 'I don't believe anyone healthy would be interested in me' becomes: 'I believe someone healthy will be interested in me.' And 'I don't want another married man' becomes: 'I want a man who is free and single.' You can read more about sending out the right energy of attraction in Chapter 5, and teach yourself how to visualize the right partner in Chapter 12. You will also find that clearing negative emotions, as we will soon do, helps you break free from the past and move towards healthier relationships.

Your Personal Psychic Session

What are your bad relationship patterns? What sort of people work with your character and who should you steer well clear of? You're going to give yourself a personal psychic session now and discover which characteristics rubbed you up the wrong way in the past and which ones will work well with your personality in the future.

To discover what these messages are, you're going to use one of my favourite techniques for tuning into relationships – tarot cards. Most people don't have their own set of tarot cards but that's OK – you can use a simple set of playing cards instead. Tarot cards and playing cards actually have very similar symbols and meanings, and some excellent clairvoyants actually prefer using playing cards so you can be assured they work just as well as a professional tarot set.

I'm always amazed by the clarity of answers given by cards. When you touch them and put your energy on them they really do work with your intuition and steer you towards the right answers. This idea may go against your logical mind, but as soon as you start working with cards you'll understand just how accurate they can be and how useful they are in opening up your intuition.

>*You're going to discover which type of person you've been attracted to in the past.*

Find a pack of playing cards, preferably a nice set, and take out the four aces. The suits each have different meanings and personalities that will help answer your question. Here are the personalities/meanings of each of the aces:

Ace of Spades: An airy, intellectual card suggesting freedom, and sometimes emotional coldness and cutting words. However, the Ace of Spades also suggests fairness and creativity, and a situation or person that inspires loyalty in others. The Ace of Spades can represent a firm and fair decision, or a challenge that requires a great deal of creativity and intellect.

Ace of Hearts: A kind, warm-hearted card that suggests a person who is changeable in spirit and can sometimes be emotionally at sea and not sure what they want. This may suggest problems with addictions, but also indicates someone who is a great listener, sensitive and understanding. As a situation, this card can represent uncertainty and plans not yet set in stone. It can also represent a decision made for emotional reasons rather than logical ones.

Ace of Diamonds: A generous card that represents everything that is down-to-earth, stable and mature. This card suggests a person who doesn't like change, works hard for a living and enjoys the creature comforts in life. The Ace of Diamonds represents someone who may not be the most optimistic or dynamic of characters but is honest and reliable. As a situation, this card can represent a decision that absolutely will not be changed. It can also indicate that someone or something is stuck in a rut and needs a helpful prod to get moving.

Ace of Clubs: A fiery, successful card that suggests someone's world has been set ablaze. Charismatic and domineering, this card suggests someone who has to be the leader and have their own way. The card suggests a real career focus, and perhaps someone who can neglect the emotional side of life so needs an independent partner. As a situation, the Ace of Clubs represents an exciting opportunity and one likely to lead to great places. It can also represent the need to stand up for yourself.

You're going to discover which type of person you've been attracted to in the past, and also which type of character is truly suited to you and will make a great partner. If you've had a mixture of good and bad relationships previously, you can use card reading to indicate which sort of person isn't right for you and discover which partner characteristics work well with your personality.

Finding Answers in the Cards

Set up a nice reading environment – perhaps in a quiet room with a candle burning and a scarf laid out to spread cards on. Shuffle the cards, closing your eyes as you do so, and think about your past relationships – particularly the things that didn't work about them. Take as long as you like doing this. When you feel a calm, loving energy wash over you, lay out the cards face down. Now run your hand over each card in turn and try to sense feelings or 'tugging' towards any one card in particular. Turn over the card you feel most drawn towards.

Look at the card and let the ideas flow towards you. Cards don't give you direct answers – that's part of their magic. They leave your intuition open to work out the answer for yourself. For example, if you turn over the Ace of Spades, your intuition might tell you that the people you've dated in the past have been a little aloof and detached, and never really committed to a serious relationship. If you turn over the Ace of Clubs, this could suggest your previous partners have been too career-orientated.

You can use the cards to help you identify past relationship patterns.

The point of tuning into your past is *not* to dwell on old relationships but to set yourself free. By calmly tuning in and getting a sense of your past relationship patterns, you'll have valuable knowledge about what doesn't work for you. But make sure you don't hold on to negative messages. Turn them into positives and tell your psychic self what you *do* want.

Now the fun part. You're going to learn what works for you in a relationship. Who is your ideal partner? Set aside your 'bad relationship' card and shuffle the cards again, this time letting your heart feel warm and thinking of love and happiness. You may want to read the rest of this chapter and learn about heart chakras to help you do this. Lay out the cards and let yourself be drawn to the person who best suits you. Remember to let any feelings and images come to you when you turn over your card. Don't only rely on my earlier descriptions – let your mind show you what it wants.

Who is perfect for you? Someone who is flighty and free (Ace of Spades), successful and independent (Ace of Clubs), grounded and generous (Ace of Diamonds) or emotional and intuitive (Ace of Hearts)?

Tom's Bad Relationship Cycle

When Tom came to me he was twenty-nine years old and very unhappy. He'd had a string of affairs with women but all of them had ended badly, and as a result Tom hated – yes, hated – the opposite sex. Whenever he went out with a woman, he felt she showed him no respect and was only after a meal ticket. As a result, he showed no respect back and the relationship quickly crumbled. Tom didn't think much of himself and believed the only worthwhile thing he brought to a relationship was his wallet. So, of course, he attracted exactly what he feared – women who were only interested in the money he would spend on them.

Together, we worked on tuning into his higher self, the positive voice inside him, and changing his negative thought pattern to something much healthier. He began telling himself, 'I want a woman who loves me for me,' and 'I am good enough to have a relationship.' Tom worked hard and made a real commitment to his psychic self. He knew he might not get results right away but was keen to keep working at it and I was proud of the effort he put in.

It took a little while for Tom to break his negative thinking, but after three months or so he began thinking in much more positive ways. On a visit to the pub with friends, he suddenly decided he didn't want to sit at the bar with the lads, drinking heavily and badmouthing women, so instead he sat with a friend he hadn't seen in a while at a quiet table. Some people turned up to meet this friend, one of whom was an old school friend of Tom's. She and Tom got talking.

This lady, Karen, was totally different from the usual women Tom went for. She was keen on family values, completely single and was calm and quiet. They began dating and Tom felt more relaxed and happy than he had done in years. His negative psychic energy had completely dissolved and he was open to the caring, healthy relationship he was now experiencing.

Clearing Negative Emotions

Do you still feel furious, hard done by or foolish when it comes to a past relationship? Perhaps you feel embarrassment when you see an ex, or hate to hear of your ex-partner getting together with someone new? This sort of negative, past-focused energy really blocks new love energy coming into your life. In order to attract a great relationship, your psychic energy needs to be positive and happy, so I'm going to show you how to get rid of negative emotional baggage.

Our emotional psychic energy is linked very much to our heart chakra – the energy spot between our ribs that holds all our feelings of love, hate and everything in between. In order to love truly, your heart chakra needs to be clear of negative feelings and unblocked, so love can easily flow in and out.

Using your heart chakra will help speed emotional answers towards you.

I'm going to show you how to open up your heart chakra, release bad feelings and let love flow freely. When your heart chakra is open and clear of negative emotions, you'll feel unconditional love flow out towards everyone – friends, enemies and exes – and this really is the best feeling in the world. People talk of a warmer, calmer, more loving energy once their heart chakra has been cleansed and opened. They no longer feel angry or want to push other people away and their capacity for relationships grows.

Your heart chakra is right at the centre of your chest, a few inches below your collarbone. It's not where your actual heart is, which is slightly to the side, but at the centre of your body. Put your hand to it now – you'll find you intuitively know the spot. This area is where you generate love, but also where all those negative emotions get stuck, blocking the free-flow of positive energy.

Opening and cleansing your heart chakra is really very simple. All you have to do is cover your heart chakra with your hand and think of something loving. This could be the love you feel for a friend or family member, or even a pet or place. As you feel love, imagine your heart chakra opening up like a beautiful, golden flower. Feel negative, dark emotions float away. You don't need the dark emotions. Only love and harmony. Tell your heart chakra that you are ready to bring in new love and feel the wave of warmth and positive energy that follows.

If you like, you can use one of the earlier techniques, such as the Psychic Staircase, to get in touch with your intuitive side whilst your heart chakra is open, and listen for any psychic messages about love or emotional blocking. Using your heart chakra to help focus your psychic meditations can make your practice much more powerful and speed emotional answers towards you.

Sit for as long as you like with your hand on your heart, letting your heart chakra open and allowing new love and peaceful feelings to flow into you. Whilst your heart chakra is open, it is impossible to allow new negative emotions in – you can only let them flow out and away. Working with your heart chakra can feel very emotional, especially if you're letting go of the past, as secretly many of us don't want to move on. Deep down, we stay attached to the past because we're a little addicted to the bad feelings and it can feel emotional to let go, especially if you're the sort of person who doesn't like change. But letting go really will bring an abundance of love into your life.

You'll experience a profound love, one that runs much deeper than surface self-esteem issues.

When you tune into your heart chakra, you might notice that at times it feels stiff and heavy and you need to wait a little while before it becomes filled with love and light. This is fine. Be patient. You might also feel uneasy at times as you're connecting deeply with your emotions. Ask your intuition about this. What emotions are being hidden and why? Ultimately, no matter what you feel when you connect with your heart chakra, the end result will be the same – a more open heart, less negative feelings and more love in your life. Surrender yourself and let your heart guide you, and your heart will truly open and be free from the bonds of the past. You'll experience a profound love, one that runs much deeper than surface self-esteem issues. It is a love that comes from your higher self and is always plentiful.

How Geraldine Opened Her Heart

One of my clients, a beautiful fifty-year-old divorcee called Geraldine, had dated many men – all of whom had been extremely jealous and controlling. She really had no idea why she was attracted to these types of men and she always thought they were nice and normal in the beginning. It was only after a few months of dating that their jealous side would begin to show.

As we talked, I discovered that Geraldine held a great deal of anger towards one of her exes – a man who had left her for another woman whilst she was pregnant. This had happened twenty years ago, but Geraldine still felt full of anger.

Unconsciously, Geraldine had been projecting this anger outwards into the psychic energy that surrounded her, and she felt completely unable to love and trust others with this negativity hanging around her. As a result, she attracted men who were just like her – angry and resentful towards the opposite sex and unable to trust. Others could sense her negative feelings but she was totally unaware she was projecting this to them. In fact, she was shocked when I told her I could sense anger coming from her psychic self.

Together we worked on opening Geraldine's heart chakra and releasing her negative emotions. This was painful for Geraldine at first, as she really didn't want to let go of the past, but finally she was able to see what a relief it would be to put down her emotional baggage and let love in.

Geraldine worked on opening her heart every day, and she was delighted to find it really did make a huge difference in her life. Within a year, she was dating someone kind and caring who trusted her completely.

One-Minute Energy Clearing

Here's a great little exercise for quickly clearing negative emotions from the past. You can use it whenever you feel anger or resentment towards an ex and it is super-effective when carried out regularly.

First, let the bad feelings come. Don't try to block them. Now say cheerfully, either out loud or to yourself: 'Thank you.' Forgive your ex for hurting you, forgive them for betraying you or causing you embarrassment. Say a great big thank you to all the pain and everything it taught you. You will feel an instant lift and release of those negative emotions, and you'll also stop the 'negative emotions snowball' from starting to roll.

The more you practise this simple little exercise, the freer and lighter you'll feel. You'll truly be amazed at how effective it is for freeing you from emotional baggage.

PART III

Tuning Into Love Matches Before You Meet

9

Psychic Wi-Fi – Tuning Into Online Love Matches

Do people really find love online? The answer is definitely yes, and when cybersurfing for a soulmate your intuitive abilities are more important than ever. I'm going to show you how to use your intuition to find the best dating websites, to create a powerful profile that attracts the right people and 'read' photos of potential online dates.

Dating websites can be a great place to meet ordinary, hard-working people who are looking for a serious relationship. However, I'm often approached by clients who are keen to find a future partner but don't want to look online. 'Aren't dating websites for hopeless cases?' they ask me. Or 'I heard dating websites are for unfaithful married men or people who can't interact in the real world.' There are horror stories about dating websites and as a matter of fact I've heard one or two of them first hand, but generally speaking websites really can be a great place to find love. The key is not to forget your intuition in the virtual world and tune into your psychic powers to keep you safe.

When you're looking for love online you do have to be

extra cautious. Inevitably there are some unscrupulous types who use Internet dating sites for a bit of fun, and there are also some people online who are downright strange. Probably there aren't many more 'bad apples' online than you would meet in real life, but when cyber-surfing for love it's easy to forget all about intuition and higher-self messages. After all, if you're sifting through lots of online profiles and messages you're looking at text and pictures. This is a very 'logical' thing to do, so often your psychic self switches off – which, of course, can lead to problems.

I'm going to show you how to tune into your intuition or 'psychic Wi-Fi' whilst you're looking for love online, and I promise if you're patient and persevere the Internet can be a great place to find a soulmate.

The Online Love Line

We're all so busy these days that our social lives often suffer, which is exactly why using the Internet can be a real boost to your dating life. Not so long ago, many people married by the time they were eighteen and marrying at twenty was considered 'leaving things a bit late', but now-adays most of us enter long-term relationships later in life and this is great. It means we know ourselves very well by the time we settle down.

The trouble is, the older we get the trickier it is to find people on our wavelength. School friends drift apart, the pool of work colleagues gets smaller as we move up the career ladder . . . Often love matches happen between friends, or friends of friends, but many of us have friends who have married or moved away, or work commitments mean we just don't go out as much as we used to.

I'm often called by clients who are lonely and want to find love, but feel a dating website is an 'unnatural' way to find a partner. This couldn't be further from the truth. What could be more natural than interacting with other single people? It happens every day all over the world. Does it matter that you don't meet people face-to-face in the first instance? Not in the slightest.

It may surprise you, but hundreds of thousands of people find long-lasting love online. In America and Canada alone, the Internet is said to have helped around 70 per cent of people find long-term relationships in recent years. Online dating is simply the modern way many hard-working people engage in the perfectly natural and age-old tradition of 'courting'.

I've counselled many clients who have found lasting marriages online. So if you haven't already looked on the World Wide Web for love, give it a try. But experienced surfer or not, use this chapter to tune into your psychic Wi-Fi, avoid the players and find the princes.

Tuning Into the Right Websites

There are thousands of dating websites out there and many attract people looking for fun, rather than serious commitment. Now, there's nothing wrong with having a bit of fun. But if you're looking for a relationship, it's important to tune into your intuition and find websites that attract other relationship-minded people or you'll most likely find yourself in emotional hot water.

We're all different, so I can't give you a list of 'good' sites to choose from (although I can tell you many of my clients have found relationships and marriage on some of the most popular dating websites). Instead, I'm going to show you how to use your psychic abilities to find sites that attract like-minded people interested in long-term love.

A World Wide Web of Choice

You wouldn't believe the number of dating websites there are out there. My clients have told me about:

- Professional/career dating websites that match people by their jobs.

- Dating websites for single parents looking for love.

- 'Marriage only' dating websites for marriage-minded people only.

- Spiritual dating sites for people interested in mind, body and spirit.

- 'Uniform' dating websites profiling fire-fighters and other uniformed professionals.

- 'Sugar daddy' dating websites for women looking for rich men.

- Army dating websites profiling single people in the army and navy.

- Dating websites for larger ladies and men only.

- 'Beautiful people only' dating websites (yes, some websites really are that shallow, and guess what – they're popular!).

- Over Fifties dating websites.

- Holiday websites that arrange weekend trips for singles.

- Same-sex dating websites.

- Love triangle websites for married people who want affairs (would you believe this is one of the top dating websites in the UK?).

Getting a Psychic Signal Online

Lots of clients come to me because they've searched for love in the wrong places online and been disappointed. If you're a single person looking for a relationship, but use dating websites where people just want a bit of fun, you'll most likely have some unhappy dating experiences. So let's tune into your intuition and discover which websites are currently attracting others interested in long-term commitment. Dating websites can attract different people from one month to the next, so what we're interested in are the sites attracting commitment-minded people right now.

I want you to take half an hour to surf the web and look at popular dating websites. It's important you're calm and relaxed when you do this, so ideally use your computer at home if you have one, or visit a pleasant and private Internet café. If you're at work with people looking over your shoulder you won't be relaxed, so make sure you take your intuition seriously and give yourself time to take a proper look online.

Using your intuition as a guide, type whatever words you like into the search engine to find dating websites, or look up any sites you've previously heard about and have caught your attention.

After half an hour or so, you should have a list of five or more sites that interest you, and your psychic alarm bells should have steered you away from sites you felt weren't attracting serious soulmate seekers.

Psychic Alarm Bells

These are a few of the psychic alarm bells that tell you a website may not be attracting people serious about long-term commitment:

- The dating website is free to join. Usually, a small monthly charge ensures all the people profiled on a site are serious about finding love.

- The people on the site have fun (and cringy) names like 'sexydave' or 'bigtom'.

- The site's online profile pictures are mainly of people doing their best to look attractive – women in full make-up and sexy outfits and men pulling their best 'I'm a stud' poses in tight jeans.

- The profiles make lots of references to being social, having fun and going out, but don't mention partnership, soulmates or long-term relationships.

Now you've weeded out the sites that aren't attracting serious relationship seekers, we're going to focus on the five or so sites you've selected and to tune into your psychic powers to find which ones match your individual needs. It could be that all five are suitable for you, but most likely two or three will match perfectly and the others won't be quite right.

Ask your intuition:
Which sites do I get the warmest feelings from?
Which sites feel like 'me' and match my personality?
On which site will I meet my soulmate?

Websites do change, so be aware that a site you choose now may change its clientele in future. Also, be somewhat wary of sites charging large sign-up fees. I've counselled several clients who've paid an absolute fortune because they thought the more they spent, the more serious a dating website would be about finding them a love match. Often, sites with high joining fees and charges are designed to attract high earners, so people in similar income brackets can find love together. But a heavy fee doesn't mean the website necessarily works harder to find you a partner, and in most cases my clients who've paid high fees have been disappointed. Don't shy away from paying a small monthly charge, though, as even a low fee tends to weed out people who aren't looking for a serious relationship.

Projecting the Perfect Profile

Now you've found one or two (or even three or four) sites that suit your needs, it's time to create the right profile. This is where your intuition can really help, as what you send out to others will greatly influence the types of dates you attract. When you listen to your psychic self, you're getting in touch with the real you – the you who will fall in love with a wonderful partner. So it's very important you tune in and listen to your higher self when creating profiles online.

How Ali's Profile Attracted Mr Wrong

When Ali came to me for advice she was using a dating website, but had been very disappointed by the experience. Having put her profile on the site, she'd attracted two men who'd taken her out to dinner, but they were both serious, formal and career-orientated types and didn't suit Ali's easy-going outlook at all. One of Ali's dates even criticized her dress sense, telling her she was 'too casual'. Ali was starting to believe that Internet dating was just too random and she'd never find the right person online.

My intuition told me Ali was attracting these mismatches, so we talked about her online profile and the information she'd written about herself. I soon discovered that Ali, who was thirty-four and retraining to be an arts therapist, was insecure about being a student so late in life. To counteract this, she had projected an image of herself as a highly professional, career-minded person as she wanted to attract a successful person and didn't want to appear too 'studenty'. Because she wasn't listening to her higher self, she'd let her insecurities do the talking and projected a false view of herself to others.

I told Ali that many people retrain later in life, and most of us view this as a very positive and brave step. Together, we rewrote her profile to reflect her true self, which was creative, free and relaxed, and soon she was attracting men who were much more on her wavelength.

Before you create your profile page, write down some keywords that describe your personality, interests and values. Don't think – instead, let your intuition do the work. Write the first things that come into your head. When you write your profile, let these words come into your self-description but also be open to new words and ideas that float in. Stay calm. Remember, you have to be honest about yourself if you're going to attract the right person. You're not trying to 'sell' yourself, you're trying to present an upbeat, honest picture of who you really are.

Be positive but be true about your values and attitudes. You're looking for romance and the right match, not just anyone. If you haven't already, you should take a look at Chapter 5 and learn how to boost your powers of attraction in order to create a powerfully positive but honest profile.

> *Professional photos can be too stiff and formal and hide your true energy.*

Now on to your profile picture. Choosing the right photo is as important as what you write, not because looks are the be all and end all but because your image sends out a powerful message about your energy and personality. You want to present yourself in a way that's truthful and appealing and lets your personality shine. Once again, your intuition will steer you in the right direction. Don't choose only 'perfect' pictures of yourself without blemishes or double chins. Instead, look over photos taken by family and friends and let your instincts tell you which ones are most positive and true of your personality.

Many people have professional photos taken and these can be very stiff and formal, with unnatural smiles, too much make-up and over-styled hair. Your energy can be hidden in these pictures. Unless you have a professional picture that you feel really represents your personality, I'd suggest choosing pictures taken by family or friends that really show your true self.

How Gemma's Photo Painted a False Picture

When Gemma got in touch with me, she wanted to know where she should look for her perfect man. She'd been using an online dating site for several months, but so far had attracted one rather odd character, one overly pushy person and lots of men who only wanted a sexual relationship with 'no ties'.

When I looked at Gemma's online profile, alarm bells went off all over the place. She'd used a very attractive, black and white picture of herself which had been taken five years previously and, although she looked good in the photo, my intuition told me she was sending out all the wrong messages. When I looked at the picture, I felt Gemma was a person who really 'loved herself' and took life too seriously. In fact, Gemma was a very quietly spoken, sweet girl who was full of self-depreciation.

I asked Gemma how she'd selected the picture and she said she'd simply picked the one that made her look the best. I explained that trying to 'sell yourself' is a fine way to cover up your true, higher self and asked her to pick three pictures that made her feel happy when she looked at them. She choose a photo of herself pulling a funny face at a party, one of her walking her dog in the park and another of her smiling with friends. In these pictures she looked natural, confident and happy, and I really got a sense of the funny, kind girl she is.

> Within a week, Gemma had been contacted by two highly suitable people who sounded very kind and genuine, and within a month she'd started dating a man who had great potential as a long-term partner.

It's a good idea to include a full body shot so people have a clear idea of who you are.

Three is the magic number when it comes to profile pictures. Choose three natural pictures of yourself, not posed but looking healthy and happy, and make sure you get a good feeling when you look at the pictures. Not an egotistical 'don't I look great' feeling, but a happy feeling inside. It's also a good idea to include a full body shot so people get a full sense of who you are. Remember – this isn't about what you *look* like as such, it's about your personality and your energy.

Psychically 'Reading' Profile Pictures

You can use your psychic abilities to intuitively 'read' the profile pictures you see online. This will help develop your psychic instincts on a deeper level and gain a whole lot more information about the people you're considering dating.

I'm sure you've heard of psychics taking a piece of jewellery or another personal belonging and using it to 'read' the personality of the person it belongs to. This is called psychometry. Psychics use photographs in a similar way to read auras and energy, and this is what I'd like to teach you to do with the online profile pictures of people you're considering dating.

The great thing about photo reading is you don't have to be highly practised or a skilled psychic practitioner to tune into your intuition and get some very powerful, strong and accurate feelings from photographs. It's a great beginner exercise, but equally many professionals use photo reading regularly. I've used this technique to get some great insights into the personalities of people my clients meet on dating websites.

Who are you interested in online? I'd like you to visit their profile page and print out a colour version of their profile picture. We're now going to use this photo to link into the person's energy and receive messages about their character and situation. You might feel a bit sceptical and wonder what on earth a photo can tell you but, believe me, you'll be amazed by what comes through.

The best way to start this process is to hold the photograph you've printed and relax your mind and body, closing your eyes and allowing images to flow in. Let your hands run over the photo as you relax, moving them from corner to corner, and really get a sense of the energy that emanates. In particular, feel the energy coming from the eyes of the photo.

If you're really good at picking up psychic energy from photos, you may well have found a new career for yourself.

As the energy begins to flow, ask yourself: 'What do I feel?' You might feel sad, happy, angry, lonely, joyful, loving or something else. You may even see people's faces, those of friends or family members perhaps. You can have your eyes open or closed whilst you let the energy come through.

Whatever comes to you, perhaps an image of a field or a black dog, or feelings of laughter or happiness, let them come. Also note the temperature. Do you feel warm and comfortable or too hot or cold? If you see or feel anything, this is a brilliant sign that your intuition is working so pay attention to whatever comes through.

Whilst you're holding the picture and feeling its energy, you can ask questions such as: 'Are you close to your family?' or 'What sort of relationship are you looking for?'

I often read photographs for clients and have had many accurate revelations over the years. I've seen images of cold, black and money when looking at a picture, only to discover the man was a compulsive gambler, and felt warm, uplifted and safe when 'reading' a man who was a kind and generous soul.

When you find out more about your potential date and discover your intuition is often accurate, you'll feel great knowing how powerful your psychic abilities can be. If you're really good and enjoy picking up psychic energy from pictures, you may well have found a new career for yourself.

If you don't experience anything at first, please don't worry. Just wait a few minutes and come back to the picture again. Remember, everyone is psychic. It's just a question of patience, practice and perseverance.

10

The Secrets of the Stars

A true understanding of star signs can boost your intuitive understanding of others and help predict your perfect partner. In this chapter, I'd like to teach you about the personality types associated with different star signs, so you'll have a better understanding of your romantic self and be more able to assess who is right for you.

When I talk about star signs, I'm referring to both sun signs and moon signs. This might be a little confusing for some of you, so let me explain. The words 'star sign' refer to the twelve signs of the zodiac (Aquarius, Pisces, etc.). However, everyone has two different star signs – a sun sign and a moon sign.

Your sun sign is what most of us commonly know as our 'star sign' or 'horoscope'. This is the sign you can read about in the newspaper each day. You're almost certainly already familiar with your sun sign and at least one or two character details related to it. Fewer of us know our moon sign, which is an equally important personality indicator and can shed much more light on why relationships may or may not work. In the next two chapters I'm going to tell you all about sun and moon signs and how they create complex and interesting personalities – and relationships. I'll also show you how to use star signs to shed intuitive light on your own character, boost your psychic abilities and find you the perfect personality match.

Do you believe in sun signs and moon signs? The truth is, it doesn't matter. When it comes to developing your intuition, it's really helpful to learn as much as you can about different personality types, whether you believe they match the sun and the moon cycles or not. This is really all horoscopes are about – personality. Learning about different characteristics and motivations can really stimulate your intuitive awareness of other people, not to mention yourself.

> *Knowing a little about your star sign, and that of your potential partner, will help you focus your intuition and open your mind.*

Personally, I'm a firm believer in sun and moon signs. I've seen enough first-hand evidence of star-sign personalities acting true-to-form in relationships. In all my years of psychic counselling I've seen many, many relationships survive and fail based on personalities that match up with sun and moon signs. That doesn't mean, however, that horoscopes are the be all and end all. They are simply a tool that can help boost your intuition and understanding of potential partners and yourself.

I don't recommend using horoscopes as the only basis for analysing a new relationship or love match potential. But knowing a little about your own star sign, and that of your potential partner, will help focus your intuition and open your mind to key personality qualities. Horoscopes won't always be the answer, but often they will enlighten you to a particular problem. For example, when I hear of a Pisces and Gemini getting together, I'm always on the look-out for mind games being played or some emotional manipulation. This doesn't mean those elements will always come into play, but I know to look out for them. Context is everything, but the stars are bright lights. They illuminate darkness and help you find even more answers about yourself and the people you're getting to know.

The Four Elements of Love

Most of us are familiar with the twelve signs of the zodiac, otherwise known as 'star signs'. Each sign of the zodiac falls under one of four elements: water, earth, air and fire. These elements shed important light on your character, especially when both your sun and moon sign elements are known.

Here are the different elements and their corresponding star signs:

- **Water**: Pisces, Cancer, Scorpio
- **Earth**: Capricorn, Taurus, Virgo
- **Air**: Aquarius, Gemini, Libra
- **Fire**: Aries, Leo, Sagittarius

Since I'm sure you already know your sun sign, check the list above to see which element matches your sunny side. Now we're going to look at the four elements, water, earth, air and fire, and learn the sorts of personality traits associated with each element. You'll be surprised how regularly the personality traits of your sun sign element match your intuitive knowledge of yourself. And, remember, in the next chapter you'll learn your moon sign and gain an even deeper insight into the elements that make up your personality.

Water Signs – Pisces, Cancer and Scorpio

If you're a water sign, you are sensitive, emotional and highly intuitive. You have great insight into emotional situations and are creative and full of imagination. When we think of water we think of emotion, depth and changeability, and these characteristics are certainly true of you if you're a water sign. You're excited by deep feelings and emotions, so love talking about relationships and bond well with people who share this passion. You have a great sense of humour too, and are a real giver in social situations and in fact all areas of life. You are a fantastic listener, which means you make a great counsellor and friend. Many water signs work in the counselling professions and help other people talk through their problems. I'm a Pisces, in case you were wondering!

Because of your highly emotional nature, you can be soft and vulnerable to criticism and on a bad day see criticism where none was intended. This is the downside of being very open with your emotions – a water sign's feelings are quite fragile and easily hurt. But this emotional openness allows you great insight into the motivations of others and gives you a fantastic ability to appreciate art, beauty and the joy in everyday life.

Make sure you take good care of yourself and say no from time to time.

Sometimes, you can appear to be secretive as well, and when you find life too threatening you retreat into yourself and hide your feelings away. This is part of your caring nature – sometimes you give too much and don't know how to say no, so end up depleting yourself and needing time alone. For a Pisces this might mean reading a book or going out to exercise alone, a Cancerian might lock themselves away in the house and a Scorpio may become rebellious and feel it's them against the world.

Another way water signs cope when the going gets tough is to indulge in addictions. Drink, drugs, gambling and sex – these are all activities water signs can get tangled up in and for anyone who has water in their chart, when the going gets tough, the addictions can get going! It's no wonder, given how much you give to others and deplete yourself, that you're more open to addictions than most. So be aware of this and make sure you take good care of yourself and say no from time to time.

When Watery Feelings Run Too Deep

As a water sign myself, I understand all too well that sometimes people under this element take things very personally. During one reading my client, whose sun was in Pisces, relayed her deep upset after being told she was 'useless at her job' by a colleague at work. She had been attracted to this colleague, so was doubly upset that he had maligned her working abilities. Knowing she was a water sign and prone to taking things personally, I dug a little deeper and discovered the man had actually said: 'The last project you worked on didn't go so well.' Not quite the same as telling her she was 'useless at her job'! She'd taken the comment in the hardest way possible, but for his part the man concerned hadn't been at all sensitive about her distress. This man had air in his sun sign, and generally wasn't known around the office for respecting the feelings of others, so I had to advise my client that although she was taking things too personally, perhaps the man wasn't for her after all. His airy side wouldn't understand her watery sensitivity.

Best Partners for Water Signs

The best matches for water signs are those who understand emotions and aren't afraid of them. Emotional water types need to surround themselves with those who understand how sensitive they are and just accept their strong emotions as part of the package of a truly wonderful, caring soul with a big heart. You're not afraid to show emotion, so it's important to find a partner who knows you need a good cry now and again.

Because you can be up one minute and down the next, it's important your partner understands your changeable emotions and provides stability. That's why earth signs often work so well with water – earthy people want to look after you, but also provide the stable base you need.

Water signs also tend not to like confrontation, so if you're in a relationship with a strong element such as fire or air, you sometimes let the other person win a little too often simply to avoid an argument. This can lead to your needs being neglected, whereas if you were with a more similar-minded personality, such as water or earth, your emotions would be more readily understood.

Best Love Matches: Any of the earth signs – Virgo, Taurus or Capricorn. Taureans spell change, and this can be inspiring for watery types. Water and water also go well together, if the pair of you can keep your emotions in check, and I've found Scorpio and Cancer and Pisces and Cancer blend particularly well.

The Perfect Partner Offers: Emotional stability, understanding and nurturing.

Relationship Challenges: You can be easily hurt and open your heart too quickly. You can also frighten other less emotional signs with your strong feelings. Tread more carefully when beginning a relationship and ask the opinion of others before taking something personally.

Earth Signs – Capricorn, Virgo and Taurus

Earth signs are strong, loyal and dependable. If you are born under an earth sign you are solid as a rock, consistent and stable. Thoroughly dependable, people know they can always rely on you to get the job done and honour your promises. Once you start something, you need a very good reason to give up before the task is completed, and this goes for relationships too – once you've made up your mind about a person, you won't be swayed and will try to make the relationship work no matter what.

Goals are very important to earth signs, particularly Capricorns. When you set a goal for yourself, you will work and work until that goal is obtained, even if everyone around you is giving up. Generally, you have a very good gauge of what's obtainable for you and know exactly which goals to add to your agenda. Which means almost 100 per cent of the time you'll achieve the goals you set, whether they're related to work or relationships.

Although not the most emotional of signs, you understand the emotions of others and provide stability during emotional storms. You like to look after other people more than you like being looked after yourself, and as a result people often turn to you in a crisis. You're a true, loyal friend and can make a long-lasting, happy partnership with the right person.

Take regular stock of your feelings and assess if your relationships are still giving you what you need.

Because you're such a great goal-setter, spontaneity often isn't at the forefront of your agenda. This isn't to say you're totally inflexible, but when you plan and set tasks you don't like being moved from your agenda and this can sometimes make you seem too independent and closed off. You're not closed off though, as you care about other people deeply, but you certainly don't want to be swayed from your path. So, yes, you can be a little stubborn. Bending to the will of others isn't in your nature if you already have a plan in place.

Sometimes people think earth signs are boring, but this really isn't true. You simply don't like change, and nor are you bothered about being the centre of attention. Often, you prefer to stay in the background or even at home, and your dislike of change means you can stick with a bad job or relationship long past its sell-by date. This can sometimes keep you stuck in an unhappy situation. Make sure you take regular stock of your feelings and assess your work and relationships. Are they giving you what you need, or are they simply familiar?

Best Partners for Earth Signs

In a relationship, earth signs need someone to help them through changes. Fear of change means you often stay in one place and miss out on life, but the right person will help push you forward and drive you to try new things. You need someone who can help shake you out of your routine, but also appreciate your need to take your time and live life at a slow, steady pace.

Dependable earth signs tend to find highly liberated

personalities, such as those associated with air and fire, rather fascinating, but you don't match well with these sorts of people. So ignore the fireworks and look for people who you can care for, without having to live life at a breakneck pace. You love taking care of sensitive people, so those who need a little looking after will suit you very well.

Try to keep an open mind when it comes to relationships, as earth signs are known for making strong decisions where romance is concerned and refusing to back down. Re-examine any romantic decisions you've made in the past and think about whether they still make sense or perhaps need to be thought over.

Best Love Matches: Any of the water signs – Pisces, Cancer or Scorpio. Earth signs work well with water signs as they nurture and understand them. I've regularly seen long-term marriages between Capricorns and Pisces, and also Virgo and Scorpio. However, in my experience, Taurians tend to work better with other earth signs.

The Perfect Partner Offers: Fun, calmness and vulnerability.

Relationship Challenges: You can be lured into mismatched relationships with highly volatile people, and in addition to this can end up staying far too long because you don't like change. You also have a bad habit of returning to familiar, but broken, relationships. Overcome your fears and step out into the unknown – I promise a better love is out there.

Air Signs – Aquarius, Gemini and Libra

The oh-not-so-boring people of the zodiac, air signs are good fun and the life and soul of the party. If you're an air sign you have the gift of the gab and love talking and entertaining people. And you certainly are entertaining. You fascinate others with your witty conversation and creative ideas. Air is changeable, like water, so you're always on the go, never stopping. You generate excitement everywhere and I guarantee any big event will be full of air signs – even ones who weren't invited! But that's fine, because you make any party or event lively and ensure there are never any uncomfortable gaps in conversation.

Because you love freedom, you may very well be self-employed. You like working your own way to your own schedule and really hate other people telling you what to do, but you can be very charming in your rejection of orders and often people don't even notice you're doing it. Most of the time, if you work for someone else, you use your gift with words to negotiate your own calendar, so you can be as free as possible and dance to your own tune.

When you do put plans into action, the results are amazing.

Because you love talking, you sometimes forget to listen, which can make you seem inconsiderate. You're not, you simply expect others to hold their own in the conversation – but it's good to remember not everyone has your gift with language.

Air signs really hate being tied down, and you like to be free to dream up your own ideas and go your own way, so you sometimes find it very difficult to follow the routes others prescribe for you. This can lead to conflict. However, despite your abundance of ideas, you can find it difficult to motivate yourself and put these ideas into practice. When you do manage to take action, though, the results are amazing.

Best Partners for Air Signs

Because you have lots of great ideas, you need motivating, energetic people around you who can generate the heat and excitement required to put plans into action. You need a partner who can understand your intellectualism and partake in lively conversation, but also give you plenty of space and freedom.

For this reason fire signs work well with air personalities because they give them plenty of freedom and heat for ideas. Air signs love the heat generated by fire signs, as this inspires them and puts their great ideas into action. I love seeing fire and air people together as this generates a real positive energy.

Air signs don't like getting too heavy, emotionally speaking, so a very intense, sensitive or emotional person isn't likely to mesh very well with you. It's not as though you lack emotions, but you like to keep things light and free. Anyone who insists on commitment early on is likely to make you run a mile and rightly so, because a clingy person will smother and frustrate you. Therefore sensitive water personalities are unlikely to suit you.

You often move from one relationship to the next without ever really getting deeply involved, so someone who is equally free and independent is an ideal partner. You need someone who understands your changeable nature and the fact you change your mind a lot. For this reason, I wouldn't recommend an earthy type of person who needs dependability and certainty.

Best Love Matches: Any of the fire signs – Leo, Aries or Sagittarius. Two air signs in a relationship can work well, but sometimes boredom can set in if they don't make an effort. The exception to this is matching Libra with Libra. As the most romantic sign of the zodiac, these two rarely run out of passion. Gemini and Libra are best of friends, and I've often seen Geminis work well with Sagittarius or Leo. Aquarius works well with Leo too.

The Perfect Partner Offers: Passion, motivation and freedom.

Relationship Challenges: You've been known to fear commitment, even with the right person, so try to overcome your phobia of being tied down and give potential partners a chance to make you happy.

Fire Signs – Aries, Leo and Sagittarius

Last but not least, we have the vibrant fire personalities. If you're born under a fire sign, you're dynamic and strong-willed and a truly great leader. Fire people are empowerers, which means you fire everyone up and get things going, ensuring work projects get underway and romance develops. You're intelligent and the most confident element of the zodiac, and bring great passion to your relationships and your working life.

If you want something, you go right out and get it and it's probably for this reason many famous people are fire signs, as they don't let rejection or competition get in their way. With so much ambition and drive, not to mention charisma and energy, it's no wonder you generally get what you want. Late nights mean nothing to you – you have bags of energy and are always able to fit in one more challenge.

> **Try to work less and make more time for relationships.**

As a natural leader, you can be quite a proud person and feel annoyed if your opinion isn't valued. You hate being ignored and love to be the centre of attention, which can lead to accusations of self-centredness. This isn't strictly true, but you do find it difficult to nurture or sympathize with people, preferring instead that they should take action themselves. Sometimes you're so busy ruling the world, you forget about emotional concerns and neglect your relationships. For this reason you can appear rather domineering, as you try to make your emotional life fit around you rather than vice versa. Try to make more time for relationships and people will realize you're not so domineering after all.

Best Partners for Fire Signs

You're hot to handle, but if someone can handle you then they're in for a passionate and exciting relationship. You need a partner who is strong enough to speak their mind, as it's very easy for you to end up walking over people who hold back their opinion. You value honesty, even if it's not pleasant, so a partner who isn't afraid to say what they think will work well with you.

Since you're very ambitious and career-minded, it's vital your partner is independent and doesn't mind spending time alone. However, at the same time, it's good for you to have a partner who can tactfully bring you out of the world of work from time to time, and into the world of love and emotions.

Because fire people get bored easily, you need a partner who is exciting and keeps you stimulated. For this reason, air types are ideal for you as they are stimulating and create exciting conversation.

Best Love Matches: Any of the air signs – Aquarius, Gemini or Libra. Other fire signs can also blend very well as heat on heat leads to excitement. Aries and Leo are a wonderful combination, one of the best, and Leo and Sagittarius can work well if one person only takes charge. The very best match is between Libra and Aries, as there is plenty of balance, passion, excitement and companionship. I wouldn't recommend fire types have relationships with a particularly sensitive water type as fire will feel suffocated and bored, whereas water will feel neglected and needy.

The Perfect Partner Offers: Excitement, independence and strong opinions.

Relationship Challenges: Fire signs can neglect relationships in favour of their career, so make sure you strike a balance between your emotional and career life. You like to lead in relationships, but remember to give romantic matches their turn at the wheel or you could generate conflict and resentment.

The Elements and Your Personality

So how can you use knowledge of the four star-sign elements in your relationships? The first thing to remember is that star signs are a guide for your intuition, not a set of rules. When it comes to star signs, nothing is set in stone and all sorts of things can affect our characters from one day to the next, such as our present life situation, moods and so on. But it is very useful to be aware that there are different types of people, be they fiery, earthy, watery or airy.

What's your elemental personality? I want you to stretch out with your feelings and intuition and match yourself to the elements you know to be true of your deeper character. I say 'elements' because many people are drawn to more than one.

More often than not, you'll find yourself drawn towards the element that matches your sun sign, but you may also find that one element alone doesn't describe you totally. If you have strong feelings towards another element, don't rule out a connection there too.

What's really interesting is that many people feel connected to two elements, and when they discover their moon sign, as you will do in the next chapter, they discover that one of the elements matches their moon sign.

As a matter of fact, it doesn't really matter if you believe these traits match up to your star signs or not (although you'll find, more often than not, they do). What's important is to understand the different personalities out there and use your intuition to discover what's true of you and what you want from a partner. We'll talk more about using star signs to discover your own relationship needs in the next chapter, once you've discovered your moon sign.

11

Moon Signs

Most people feel a connection to their sun sign element, but equally you may have an instinct that this element alone doesn't paint a full picture of your personality. This is probably because you haven't taken your moon sign into account. Your moon sign may be very different from your sun sign and it can really help shed light on your personality, and show what you need from potential partners.

What is a moon sign and why is it important for your relationships? The moon typically depicts anything emotional, shadowy and mysterious, so moon signs are said to express your true emotional personality. Sun signs, on the other hand (the traditional 'star signs' that you read in the paper) and their elements are said to describe your individuality.

Very often, I notice people are more like the element (fire, water, earth or air) that matches their moon sign than their sun sign. Many of my clients will tell me their sun sign without me having to ask, but it's only when I probe deeper and discover their moon sign and its corresponding element that I have a full set of psychic tools with which to understand their personality.

Moon signs are especially important when it comes to relationships, as they reflect our emotions and feelings. Your sun sign might be in airy, independent Aquarius, but if your moon is in watery, sensitive Cancer, you may require a lot of compassion and understanding in a relationship. Your moon sign essentially governs how you behave in relationships and friendships, and really where any emotional attachments are concerned. Discovering your moon sign opens up a whole new understanding of love and emotions – your own and other people's.

Calculating Your Moon Sign

So let's discover your moon sign. You may be in for quite a surprise, as moon signs are commonly related to a completely different element than your sun sign. Those who thought they were fiery may well discover a watery core, and airy-fairy sun signs might find they are actually very earthy and reliable underneath. The same goes for any potential love matches. You may have already learned the sun sign of your love match, but see a completely different picture when their moon sign comes to light.

Calculating your moon sign is fairly simple. You need your date of birth and your birth time. Easy to discover about yourself, but perhaps a little bit more difficult to find out about anyone you're dating!

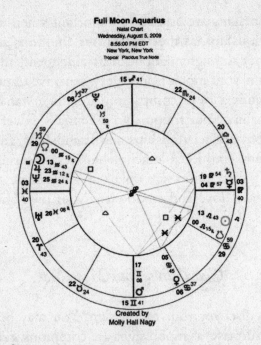

Full Moon Aquarius
Natal Chart
Wednesday, August 5, 2009
8:55:00 PM EDT
New York, New York
Tropical Placidus True Node

Created by
Molly Hall Nagy

Now you've discovered your moon sign, romance is about to get much more interesting. If you haven't already, I'd like you to look at the four elements (water, earth, air and fire) in the previous chapter and read about your moon element – the one that matches your moon sign. It could be that your moon element is the same as your sun element, in which case you're a very strong and true representation of that element. Water types will be even more sensitive and giving, whereas fire personalities will have even more confidence and dynamism. However, you could find a brand new element that unlocks an extra layer of understanding about your personality.

Your Love Match's Moon Sign

There's absolutely nothing wrong with using horoscopes to help your intuition figure someone out, but ask a first date their birth date (not to mention the time of their birth!) and they'll think you've already planned the wedding and will probably run for the hills. Nothing scares people off faster than thinking they're being assessed for serious long-term potential, so save the horoscope questions for when you're in a serious relationship.

However, it's fairly easy to find out someone's star sign without looking like a bunny boiler. Simply bring up the topic of birthdays and, chances are, before long they'll tell you when theirs is. Check the moon chart and you may be able to tell their moon sign, or at the very least have a choice of two moon signs. Your intuition will tell you the right one.

If Your Moon Element Matches Your Sun Element . . .

If your moon element is the same as your sun element, your personality will be an even stronger, truer version of that element. So, for example, if your sun sign is Libra (air) and your moon sign is Gemini (also air), your personality will have strong doses of creativity, charm and flightiness. You might be even more inclined to dance in and out of relationships and fear commitment, but on the positive side you're especially charismatic and are able to form relationships easily. If you're a doubly earthy personality, you might need even more help getting out of a romantic rut, but you're one of the most loyal people around and will be utterly committed to whomever you have a relationship with. Two water signs in your chart? Your powers of intuition are highly tuned, but you can be a little sensitive and take things too personally. And if you have double fire in your horoscope, well, watch out everyone, because you'll be charging forward setting the world alight. But remember to keep an eye on your domineering side as it sometimes rubs people up the wrong way.

So what does a double element mean for relationships? First, it's important to understand that the challenging sides of your element are likely to be doubly true of you. You need to be extra aware of your more challenging qualities to keep you balanced and make sure you don't fall victim to being too extreme. Second, it's extra important to be around people who complement your powerful characteristics and understand your true nature.

Take a second look at the challenging qualities of your element. Now I'd like you to get in touch with your intuition and ask:

Who do I know who understands this and accepts this about me?

Think of friends, relatives and past partners who really appreciated your challenging side and knew how to deal with it. These are the sorts of people you need in your life.

Double Trouble

I remember very well doing a psychic reading for a lady whose sun was in Cancer and whose moon was in Pisces. She was a very sensitive and caring person who was beginning a relationship with a Leo man. Straight away I was on the alert for this fiery person causing friction, and in fact on their first date this lady told me the man seemed quite full of himself and wouldn't let her get a word in edgeways. A typical water sign, she went along with it. I let my intuition go to work and felt strongly that this man's moon sign was also fiery, and that this lady should really take care. We soon discovered that the man's moon was in Sagittarius – double fire! As their relationship progressed, this lady fell head over heels in love. She was certain this fiery man was the one, but my instincts still told her to be cautious. It turned out he was a two-timing, egotistical rat-bag and she was badly hurt. So a word of warning: if you have double elements in your chart, be doubly careful to avoid your wrong match!

If Your Moon and Sun are Two Different Elements . . .

If you have two different elements in your chart, for example a water sun sign and a fire moon sign, you'll have a real range of romantic qualities which make you complex, interesting and sometimes a little bit difficult to understand. You may even have difficulty understanding yourself sometimes. The good news is, once you've read and understood your two different elements, you'll have a clearer picture of what you really need in a relationship, and because of your double elements you can potentially relate well to a broad range of people.

When you have two different elements in your sign, your major obstacle is understanding yourself and your own needs. You've probably known your sun sign all your life, but most of us never bring in our moon element or understand just how important this part of the horoscope is in understanding our personality. No wonder love can be confusing.

I want you to use your intuition now and really feel your way into your unique personality and needs. These are the questions I want you to ask your higher self:

What are my three biggest relationship needs?

What sort of person will provide these needs?

What are the three main qualities of people who understand me and bring harmony?

Use any one of the psychic exercises from Part I to get in touch with your higher self and answer these important questions. They will give you a far greater understanding into the complex wonder that is you, and put you on a great path to visualizing a partner.

Perfect Balance

One of my clients, Kerry, met a Libran man at work and they began seeing each other for dinner a few times a week. Kerry really liked Mark, but she was worried he might not be ready to settle down and that she would be too needy for him. Kerry is a Pisces, so if I had only used her sun sign to boost my intuitive understanding of her situation, I would have been alert for her watery sensitivity frightening off an airy Libran who didn't want to fall into feelings too deeply. But Kerry's moon was in Aries, a fiery personality that excites and stimulates airy people. And Mark's moon sign was in Cancer, which gave him watery characteristics that helped him understand Kerry's sensitive side. As we worked together, a picture began to form of a very well-balanced match, and as time went on Kerry and Mark got closer. After two years of dating, they were married and have remained together, happily so, for five years.

When you have two different elements in your sign, the key is to understand yourself and then find a partner who understands you. Using your knowledge of the elements and your intuition, you can gain a great deal of understanding about your romantic self and get a much clearer picture of the perfect partner who understands your needs. For example, if you have fire and earth in your personality, you may discover a previously unrealized domineering side that needs to be kept in check, but also understood by a partner – perhaps someone with fire or air in their personality who can handle this sort of behaviour. We all have moments when we're at our worst, and it's during these times we really need a partner who understands and appreciates us.

Using the Stars to Attract the Perfect Partner

So how can moon (and sun) elements help you understand yourself and what you need from a relationship? Appreciating the elements of your character will give you a much clearer picture of what you need romantically and hone your visualization powers to bring you the perfect person.

Perhaps you hadn't noticed this before, but I bet your friends' sun and moon elements complement yours very well. Think of your best friends and their corresponding sun elements. Find out their moon elements if you can. It really should be no surprise that the majority of your friends will share your element/s or be born under elements that work well with yours.

Romantic relationships can be exciting, passionate, scary and fun, but it's important to remember that we already have lots of strong relationships in our lives – with friends and family. Those of you who worry about being single may do well to remember this. No one is truly alone, we all have people who care about us and understand who we really are, even if we're not in a romantic relationship.

The good relationships we have with our friends and family are important because they teach us the basis of what we need in romantic relationships and help steer us towards what we really need in a partner. After all, the best romantic relationships are built on friendships – if you can't be friends with a partner then you can't be much of anything.

Think of the person, friend or family member, who you enjoy your best and closest relationship with. What are their sun and moon elements? Now ask your intuition:

What is it about this person's personality that blends so well with mine?

How about the people you don't get on so well with? We all have them. Work colleagues and even close friends sometimes rub us up the wrong way. What are the sun and moon elements of these people? Now ask your intuition:

What is it about this person's personality that doesn't work with mine?

You can use the four elements described in the previous chapter as a guide to these personality complements and clashes, but don't let these ideas suffocate your natural psychic abilities. You *know* what works for you and what doesn't. It's just a case of tuning in and finding out.

Using Star Signs to Test Your Intuition

This is a really fun exercise to hone your psychic powers and help you get in touch with your intuition quickly. First, think of a person you know reasonably well but whose birthday you don't know. You might choose a colleague at work, your hairdresser, a friend of a friend or someone else.

Unless you have an excellent knowledge of star signs, it's hard, especially for a beginner, to pinpoint someone's sun and moon signs. So I'm not going to ask you to do that. Instead, you're going to try and guess sun and moon *elements* – water, earth, air or fire. Of course, if you have a strong, intuitive feeling that a particular sign matches a person, feel free to go with it. But you'll find it easier to tune into your feelings about particular elements rather than the signs themselves, which are rather complex and varied.

Does the person have a sensitive side? Are they fiery and charismatic, creative and intellectual or dependable and down-to-earth? What do your feelings tell you about the person? If no strong feelings come to you, snap your fingers and say the first one or two elements that come into your head.

Next time you meet the person, find out their birthday and (if possible) birth time and see if you were right. This is a bit like a party game and it is lots of fun to play it at parties, but don't discount its validity as an exercise for boosting your psychic abilities. It's a brilliant way to practise tuning into people, with the added bonus that you get a proven result at the end to see if your intuition was right.

12

Using Clairvoyance to 'See' Your Soulmate

In this chapter, you're going to learn some real mind magic as I'm going to show you how to see into the future. As a clairvoyant, I'm often asked to gaze into my crystal ball (figuratively speaking) and tell my single clients if there is a 'tall handsome stranger' on the horizon. Inevitably, I tell them: 'Well, that depends on you.'

I believe we all have the power to create love in the future. I call this 'creative clairvoyance'. Creative clairvoyance is something you can do right now to bring about a happy, loving destiny for yourself. Your future is not set in stone. We all have the ability to both see the future and create the future, and our destinies can be changed and improved. The purpose of our future-seeing talent is both to steer you away from a bad course and create a wonderful life for yourself.

You have the power to bring love into your life. It's just a question of unlocking your abilities to see the *right* future and then bring it to pass. Together, we're going to work on creating a strong image of your soulmate and your future relationship, and then use your psychic power to make this a reality.

Ready to Meet Your Soulmate?

No matter how many bad relationships you've had in the past or how long you've been single, I promise there is a perfect partner in your future. All you need to do is focus your mind and find out who they are. This isn't trickery or make-believe. Your soulmate is hovering in the psychic shadows of destiny, and you're going to use the power of your mind to bring them into focus and into your life.

Many people don't realize just how powerful their psychic abilities are when it comes to attracting partners. When we don't understand how creative clairvoyance creates partners for us, we don't focus our mind. We have a vague picture of who we want and we project these unfocused images into our future. Instead of creating the right relationship for ourselves, we let our cloudy minds bring cloudy people into our lives and hearts – people who may not be right for us. It's like swimming in a stormy, foggy sea. When you can't see properly, you're likely to grab hold of the first tatty lifebuoy you see and miss the big, beautiful ship sailing past. I don't want you summoning just anyone into your future. It's very important you see and attract the right person if you're to have a happy, long-lasting relationship.

Creative clairvoyance is extremely powerful when it comes to love and romance. Many of us unconsciously use our psychic abilities to 'see' and attract the wrong people, which is why I'm contacted by so many clients in bad relationships. They used their mind to project the wrong partner into the future and hey presto – they get them.

How Clive Created the Wrong Future

I often hear from clients who've inadvertently used their psychic powers to create the wrong future for themselves. Without realizing it, they've projected a 'negative' of the future and by picturing it over and over again have attracted this negative into their lives. I want to share with you now the story of one of my clients who did just that, so you can understand just how important it is to take control of your future thinking and project the right images into your life.

Clive had just come out of a year-long serious relationship when he contacted me. His girlfriend, Vanessa, had left him for one of his closest friends and he felt angry and betrayed, but explained that he wasn't really surprised. He'd always been certain, he told me, that Vanessa would leave him for another man. In fact, he'd told her repeatedly during the relationship: 'I'm sure one day you'll leave me for someone else.'

As we talked more, Clive told me he'd never really felt good enough for Vanessa, whose family were very affluent and well-known in the world of business. However, my intuition told me different. I sensed he was in fact very successful in his field and, not only that, he was kind, honest and reliable. He soon confirmed that he ran a profitable engineering business and had made a great deal of effort in his relationship.

The trouble was, Clive didn't think enough of himself. He had always been sure Vanessa was too good for him and believed she deserved better. The deeper they got into the relationship, the more Clive worried and the more he expressed these worries to Vanessa. 'I'm sure you'll find someone better and leave me,' he told her over and over again. Without realizing it, he was painting a bleak future for himself and casting Vanessa as the unfeeling villain.

When Vanessa left him, Clive said to her, 'I told you this would happen,' at which point this poor lady, who had really been pushed by Clive into ending the relationship, left for good. Clive got exactly what he predicted for himself.

What future are you creating for yourself right now?

Whenever I counsel clients, I'm always amazed by how few of them have actually taken the time to consider who their perfect partner is. They often know very well what doesn't work, but they've never really sat down and visualized Mr Right. We're going to do that right now, because creating a strong image of your perfect partner will bring a loving, supportive, caring person into your future.

The Three Doors to the Future

Who is your perfect partner? We're going to go beyond looks, income and sex appeal and also totally ignore what other people might say or think about who is right for you. You're going to fine-tune and focus on the partner, the soulmate, who will fill you with happiness and work with you to create a long-lasting partnership.

There are three doors to your future, and once you've unlocked all three of them I promise it's only a matter of time before your soulmate walks into your life.

Door One: The Power of One Hundred

'The Power of One Hundred' is a psychic tool I use with clients to fine tune their image of a perfect partner. Using it will put you on the path to projecting a perfect partner in your future. I've used the 'Power of One Hundred' on many, many occasions to help clients unlock a happy, loving destiny. It is an excellent way to bring your soulmate out of the shadows and into your life – and it's very simple to do.

Take a large, lined piece of paper and write out at least a hundred things you would like in your future partner. Use only one piece of paper. If the paper gets full, turn it over or squeeze sentences in any white space that's left. You can write more than a hundred qualities if you wish – and remember: this is your list and you can write whatever you like, no matter how silly or trivial.

You may be thinking, 'I'm not sure I can think of a hundred things.' Trust me, you will once you get going. There is a good reason why I'm asking you to write so many qualities. It's because I want you to overtake your logical mind and access your psychic self. Your psychic self can sound a little bit silly sometimes. It can sound insignificant too. Or vain. Sometimes childish. You may find yourself writing 'qualities' such as: 'loves watching *EastEnders*', 'has a tattoo', 'has really smooth skin', 'can ride a bike with no hands'. It doesn't matter what you write, as long as you mean it. Anything goes. Absolutely anything. There is nothing too trivial or too silly to go on the list. Equally, there is nothing too serious. No one else needs to see the list but you, so really let yourself go and let your higher self speak through you.

> *Once you've written a hundred qualities about your perfect partner, you'll have a powerful picture of your soulmate.*

Sometimes, clients get very confused when I ask them to conjure up qualities of an ideal, loving partner. This is because they're trying to please others in their choice of partner – perhaps friends or family, or even society. They want to fit in and have a 'normal' relationship. Some people feel a lot of pressure to settle down with a particular sort of person because it is expected of them. For example, they might feel a need to settle down with a partner who earns a good salary. Or the expectation might be that a 'good' partner owns their own home or looks a certain way. The expectations of others can really cloud your judgement of what makes a perfect match, but ultimately you need to think of the partner who is right for you and **makes you happy**.

Clients will sometimes list qualities they tell me are very important in a partner – income, looks, education level – but I can tell they feel no joy when they're expressing these ideas. What makes you feel joyful when you think of a future partner? What are the qualities that really excite you and make you come alive?

Don't write negative things such as 'doesn't treat me badly' or 'won't leave me for someone else'. Your psychic mind can have a powerful effect on your future and I don't want any negativity coming along for the ride. Write positive statements only. Tell the future what you want and your psychic self will begin moving aside the shadows and bringing your soulmate into focus.

Once you've written the list, keep it with you – perhaps in a secret pocket in your bag or coat. Or maybe a special keepsake box or wardrobe at home if you're worried about others stumbling across it. But it's very important to keep the list somewhere personal to you, so either on your person or among personal objects.

You'll find once you've written your hundred qualities you will have a powerful picture of the person you want to spend the rest of your life with. And, believe it or not, that person exists in your romantic future and is flowing towards you right now. Your soulmate might be a totally new person or an old friend who drifts back into your life at exactly the right moment. But, whoever they are, you can be certain they have the qualities you're looking for.

Door Two: Your Psychic Mood Board

By writing your 'One Hundred' list you've given yourself a much clearer picture of your soulmate. And you've sent a powerful message about what you'd like in a relationship. Now we're going to work on unlocking the second door to a loving future, which means helping you picture your life and soul merging with your future partner's.

To bond the two of you together with love, we're going to use a technique called a 'psychic mood board'. Many psychics use mood boards to see into the future and visualize what they want to come to pass, and now you're going to do the same thing.

Mood boards are a lot like the old collages you might have made at school. Using cut-out pictures, paints, hand drawings and words, you're going to create a beautiful representation of you and your soulmate together. This image will help you secure love in your mind and project it into the future.

First, choose ten things that represent you. They can be words, colours, photographs, pictures of something like shoes, pets, flowers, book covers, film posters and DVDs – really anything at all, but you must be able to draw them, write them or cut or print them out, as you're going to glue them to your mood board.

Next, choose ten things from your 'One Hundred' list that best represent your partner – the things that are most important to you. Spend a bit of time considering the ten words that really sum up your soulmate, then think about how you're going to represent these words in a picture. For example, if you've chosen 'really tidy around the home' (are you a Virgo by any chance?) you could write the word 'tidy' or you could find a picture of a broom or a sparkling-clean kitchen. Whatever works for you.

Now buy a large sheet of rose or red-coloured paper from an arts and craft shop, together with any sprinkles and sparkles you fancy, and stick your twenty items to the card, making sure they're mixed up and merged together. You might want to add inspiring words like 'love' and 'soulmate' around the pictures and fragrance the board with your favourite perfume.

Some of my more independently-minded clients like to keep their pictures and their partner's pictures reasonably separate on their mood boards and this is fine. But make sure they're not too separate – a relationship is about sharing your life with someone else, not co-existing at a distance.

Your mood board will create a bit of magic in your future.

If you're thinking all this sounds like playing around and making a mess, you're right. Your psychic self loves fun and games, and remember, it's your psychic self who will project the right partner into your future.

Once your love mood board has been completed, keep it in a safe place where it won't get dusty or torn. Again, you don't have to show this to anyone – it's just for you. You can use mood boards for anything, from projecting a great career in your future to finding the perfect home, but love is the area in which mood boards work best because it's an area of life that has such a strong emotional charge.

This isn't a process to rush so I don't want you to try and complete your mood board in an hour or even over a few days. You're going to spend the next week or so looking for creative inspiration in the things around you. This includes magazines and books, websites, leaflets and TV programmes.

Without you having to do anything at all, your finished mood board will create a bit of magic in your future. It will bring a wonderful relationship into your life – all you have to do is believe in yourself and the power of your creative clairvoyant abilities.

How Selina Created her Soulmate

A few years ago, I was contacted by a quiet, reserved lady in her mid twenties. She was a very sweet person with lots of friends, but had unfortunately been unsuccessful with men. She was attractive, both in looks and personality, and had a really caring energy, but the trouble was she didn't know what she wanted in a partner and therefore her clairvoyant mind, the part of her that wanted to make a wonderful future, had no idea what to create for her. This meant it created nothing at all and Selina had relationships with entirely the wrong people.

Together we thought about potential partners that would suit her personality. I could sense Selina was a sensitive soul, but also highly independent, so we considered the sort of person who would complement these characteristics. Then I asked Selina to get passionate and think about what, in an ideal world, she'd love in a relationship. As her homework, I asked her to create a mood board and she really excelled herself, making a wonderful collage of pictures framed with rose petals and fragranced with lemon oil.

We worked on a series of affirmations to go with the pictures, and these were:

I am happily married.
I am with my soulmate.
I am happy in love.
My partner loves me.

Selina spoke these affirmations out loud whilst looking at her mood board each day. She did this for a number of weeks. After that, she put the mood board away and forgot all about it until a few months later, when she and an old family friend, a friend who matched many of the qualities on her mood board, struck up a romance. I was surprised to receive a call from Selina telling me she was getting married – only six months after we'd worked on her mood board together. She told me she'd looked at the mood board again after her fiancé proposed and was completely overwhelmed by how closely her pictures matched the man she was going to marry.

Door Three: Your Love Story

Your mind is such a powerful source of energy that it really can create a fantastic, loving future for you – provided it has positive images and thoughts. The final door to destiny is about writing a great love story for youself, so you can give your clairvoyant mind strong images and begin willing things into reality. We've already sent some powerful messages out about the type of partner you'd like to attract and how this partner will merge with your life. Now we're going to bring about your future relationship in full detail, using lots of positive emotions to tune into your psychic side and tap into your creative clairvoyance.

When it comes to creating the future, your clairvoyant mind only needs a goal. It doesn't need a road map or instructions about how to get somewhere. I don't want you worrying about the 'hows'. What your destiny really cares about is your destination. So your love story is going to describe your relationship destination in fantastic colour and detail. I want you to tell me about you and your future partner. Breathe deeply, find a quiet place and ask your intuition:

What do my partner and I like to do together?
How do we talk to one another and what sort of conversations do we have?
How does my partner look at me?
What do I love most about my partner?

The answers to these questions will provide words and pictures for your love story. Here is the love story of one of my clients, Cassie, who is now living with a long-term boyfriend. She wrote this love story two weeks before she and her partner met:

> *My partner is my soulmate and best friend. He treats me with complete respect and is a very loving and spiritual individual. We share a wonderful home and our favourite place is the kitchen, where my partner cooks the most amaz-ing meals. He is honest, faithful and grounded, and I can honestly say I've never felt more secure or cared for until now. We understand each other totally and can often communicate without words. Happiness is spending time together.*

Cassie's boyfriend is a food enthusiast who worships the ground she walks on, cares for her and their home, and they really do have a wonderful life together. She can't believe her love story had such powerful results, and she's kept the crinkled piece of paper to show friends how important the psychic mind can be.

So now you're going to write your love story. You can write much more than Cassie, or keep it short and simple, but when you read it I want you to feel uplifted and happy. Don't write more than one draft, but take your time and let your psychic mind do the talking.

You'll find that now you've really focused on your perfect partner and your future relationship, you'll feel much more relaxed and secure about your destiny. You'll have a strong feeling inside that your perfect relationship *will* come to pass. It's simply a question of waiting for destiny to unfold. This doesn't mean that the very next person you meet romantically will be 'the one', or that you should ignore any psychic alarm bells ringing, but you should know that true love is on its way for you and when the time is right your perfect partner will arrive.

PART IV

First Encounters – Mind Reading When You Meet

13

Grounding Before a First Encounter

How do you feel during the few hours before a date? Calm and centred, or sick with nerves? When you meet someone romantically, how you feel beforehand can make a big difference to your experience. If you feel mainly happy and relaxed, it's likely your romantic encounter will go smoothly and enjoyably, and you'll be in the right frame of mind to hear any psychic messages from your higher self. If you feel nervous and negative, you'll smother your intuition and probably send out negative signals when you meet your date.

Now, of course, you wouldn't be human if you didn't feel some anxiety before a date, especially if you don't know your romantic match very well. Dates are often in new places with new people and it's human nature to fear the unknown. I don't expect you to magically transform into a serene, angelically calm figure – it's not necessary to be 100 per cent calm to enjoy dating and send out positive psychic energy. But what I can show you is how to work with techniques used by top psychics to make you feel more relaxed and 'grounded' before a date. My clients who work on 'grounding' themselves have more positive dating experiences and tend to find the right relationships much more quickly.

First, we're going to work with your psychic self to answer any uncertainties before a first date, so you feel confident about what to expect when you meet your love match. Then I'm going to show you how psychics 'ground' themselves, using the power of the earth to calm body, mind and spirit.

First Date Fears

Dating should be lots of fun, but many people are so anxious they find it impossible to relax and enjoy themselves before and during a first date. This is perfectly understandable. It is simply fear of the unknown.

If you're meeting a blind date or someone you met on the Internet, it's nerve-racking as you have no idea what to expect. Equally, if you already know your date and are very keen on them, this can be intimidating as you really want things to go well. Some of my clients have experienced truly awful dates in the past and this can also add to pre-date butterflies. A final common concern, which may sound insignificant but certainly isn't, is not knowing much about the date venue. Clients tell me they're worried they'll dress or behave wrongly and feel embarrassed, and this is a very understandable worry.

All these anxieties, which largely come down to a fear of the unknown, can be reduced by talking to your psychic self before a date. You can use a mixture of divination and creative clairvoyance to answer any questions you have and project a positive vision of your date experience into the future. Let's work through the most common dating concerns one by one.

'I've never met my date before and have no idea what to expect'
It's perfectly natural to feel nervous about meeting someone new, especially if you're going on a blind date and don't even know what your date looks like. But your psychic self can tell you lots before your romantic encounter. The answers are inside you just waiting to come out.

If you've met your date on the Internet and have a picture of them, carry out the photo-reading exercise in Chapter 9 to find out as much as you can about them. Try, if you can, to find out your date's sun and moon signs before the date too (Chapters 10 and 11), so you can gain some insight into their character. Finally, carry out the Psychic Staircase exercise in Chapter 2 and ask your psychic self to show you the person you are meeting at the bottom of the staircase. Then you can interact with your date before you meet and find out more about what sort of person they are.

If you're going on a blind date, ask your psychic self to reveal what your date will be wearing, their posture and hair colour, so you feel less anxious about identifying the 'man with the pink carnation'.

'I really like the person I'm meeting so it's very important things go well'
Great! It's wonderful you think there may be a future with your date. But see what your psychic self has to say too. Get calm and ask your intuition 'Does this person really

have potential?' and let colours flash up, red for no, green for yes, to double-check you're really on the right track. If red flashes up, be extra alert for any psychic alarm bells during your date.

If you're nervous because you really like your date, it's particularly important to get in touch with the right psychic energy and positive thinking before you meet to make sure you're giving out the right signals. Read about your 'Power of Attraction' in Chapter 5 and you can also employ the creative clairvoyance technique outlined in Chapter 12 to picture your date going smoothly.

'I've had bad dates before and I just can't imagine this one going well'

It makes sense to feel nervous if you're anticipating a bad experience and, of course, if you've had lots of bad dates you're likely to be expecting more of the same. This is a really negative cycle I've seen lots of my clients get stuck in, and the solution is simply to work with your psychic clairvoyant side to project a great date in your future. Use the creative clairvoyance discussed in Chapter 12 to picture a wonderful dating scenario for yourself and say the affirmation, '*I'm looking forward to a great date,*' a few hours before your romantic meeting.

'I don't know much about where we're going and I'm worried I'll get things wrong and be socially awkward'

This is a classic dating concern and often people feel silly about and don't take seriously. But if you don't acknowledge it, your psychic self can't help you. When you go to a new place it can be nerve-racking and if you don't know the person you're meeting very well, this can really raise the anxiety levels. Nobody wants to do the wrong thing and feel embarrassed in front of someone they're getting to know. But your psychic self can help. You can get a wonderful sense of the energy of a place by tuning into your psychic abilities.

Before your date, ask your psychic self to give more details about where you're going. Use the Psychic Staircase exercise and ask your intuition: '*Show me the sort of place I'm going to visit and let me feel the energy it gives out.*' You may also want to ask: '*What's the best outfit to wear to this venue?*' and '*What tips can you give me about enjoying myself in this new place?*'

Using your psychic self, you can really help spill light on the unknown and make yourself feel much safer and more comfortable. However, you can't always know what's coming in life, even if you are in tune with your psychic self, so it's also important to feel generally calm and secure before an encounter. This is what I'm going to show you how to do next.

How the Earth Gives Calming Energy

You're now going to learn how to use the calming powers of the earth to relax yourself before a date. Have you noticed that when people are feeling lonely, frightened or sorry for themselves, they tend to stare at the ground?

Subconsciously, they are trying to feel more secure by 'grounding' themselves. And it works. Mother Earth has amazing powers when it comes to keeping us calm and focused. When we think of soil, grass and even concrete, it makes us feel safer and less vulnerable. Psychics know this and often use earth-related techniques to calm them before a high-profile event or encounter.

Looking down at the ground may be a quick fix if you're feeling insecure, but it sends out totally the wrong psychic signals to your date and cuts off any intuitive links you might build between the two of you. The key is to fill yourself with the soothing, safe energy of the earth and then use a releasing technique to boost your confidence and fill yourself with more lively, sociable 'air' energy.

You're now going to learn a two-part technique that anchors you to the relaxing powers of the earth, and then releases you so you're ready to face the world with calmness and confidence.

First Stage: Courage From the Earth

I'm going to tell you about a very powerful anchoring technique that can be used before dates, job interviews, exams – really any situation that's likely to make you feel nervous beforehand.

Whenever we're nervous, we feel out of control and negative thoughts can start to creep in, no matter how positive we usually are. I've known clients worry endlessly before dates and, of course, when you're worried you're totally disconnected from both yourself and the world outside. This anchoring technique, which I call 'Courage from the Earth', will show you how to reduce nerves considerably, no matter what situation you're facing.

It's good to practise this technique a few times before you try it out for real, because once you feel how truly effective it is this knowledge in itself will relieve some of your anxiety before a date. In fact, one of my clients told me that as soon as I taught her 'Courage from the Earth' she felt much calmer, even without putting the technique into practice. Just the knowledge that she had this powerful tool to help her made all the difference.

So I'd like you to gain 'Courage from the Earth' now. A truly wonderful place to carry out this technique is in the garden with your shoes off, especially in a patch of raw soil, but this isn't always possible and it certainly isn't necessary to feel grounded. Read all the instructions through once before trying out the exercise:

1. Stand up and look at the ground. It doesn't matter where you are – even if you're standing on thick carpet on the third floor of a building you can still feel a connection with Mother Earth simply by turning your focus downwards.
2. Either take off your shoes or stamp your feet to feel the ground beneath you. Feel how solid and dependable it is. How certain and safe.
3. Now imagine you're rooted to the ground. Your feet are completely part of whatever you're standing on and your body feels as solid as a tree trunk.

4. Let your mind wander over each part of your body in turn, feet, calves, legs and so on, right up to your neck, and as you experience each part of your body really feel how heavily connected to the ground you are. Feel weight pulling you downwards.

5. Pat your body, as you would with a towel when you've just come out of the shower, and feel how solid your body is and how safely you're resting on the earth.

6. Say to yourself, either out loud or in your head: *'The earth soothes and protects me. As long as I am on the earth, I am always calm and safe.'*

It really is amazing how this technique can instantly lower your stress levels and remind you how solid and safe things really are. You have nothing to fear. Everything is OK and, just as the ground is always below, so your psychic self is always there to guide and protect you.

How Fiona's Grounding Ended Her Anxiety

Fiona contacted me after many years of terrible dating experiences. She was a very attractive lady in her forties who had met lots and lots of men on dates, but rarely got past the second date stage. If she did, she inevitably found out the man was married or not looking for a long-term commitment. Fiona felt like a hamster stuck in a wheel, going over the same bad dates again and again, and she worked herself up into such a state of anxiety before her dates that she was thinking about stopping dating altogether.

'What's the point?' she asked me. 'I feel so nervous before the date that sometimes it makes me sick, and then when I get there I have an awful time and usually end up getting rejected.' I asked Fiona what she usually did before a date, and she told me she spent hours getting ready, all the while worrying about what her date would think of her and all the things that had gone wrong in the past. The main thing she thought before a date was: 'Oh, this will be the same as before and I'll end up being single.' A positive outlook if ever there was one! Of course, she was sending powerful signals to her creative clairvoyant self to build a negative experience for her, but that wasn't all. She was also making herself feel frightened and apprehensive before every date, and this was having very negative consequences. It meant she was sending out closed-off signals to the men she met and also her psychic self wasn't able to pick up on any alarm bells.

I talked Fiona through the 'Courage from the Earth' exercise and, although she was sceptical, she agreed to try it out before her next date, which happened to be that evening. Fiona got so anxious before dates she was sure nothing could make her feel relaxed, but I encouraged her to have faith and she agreed to try.

During the grounding exercise, I asked Fiona to say to herself: *'I'm going to have a great time tonight — I'm sure he'll be a nice guy no matter what happens.'*

The date went far better than Fiona had hoped, and she told me it was the best experience she'd had in years. The man in question wasn't for her, but because she'd felt calm and in control she'd noticed the warning signs (phone calls from his 'ex'-girlfriend during the meal that he just had to run off and take) and just enjoyed the evening for what it was — a nice meal out with a man.

The more Fiona carried out the grounding exercise, the more she noticed she was getting past the second-date stage with different sorts of men — calmer, nicer men who were caring and attentive towards her and wanted commitment. She began to really enjoy dating and instead of feeling anxious she felt excited before new romantic meetings.

As her confidence grew, Fiona couldn't believe there had been a time when she was thinking of stopping dating altogether.

Second Stage: Sociability From the Air

Grounding makes you feel safe, but when you're on a date you need to have equal contact with the earth (safety) and air (sociability), otherwise you won't be able to connect with your date on any level at all, let alone a psychic one. You try having a conversation with someone fixated on the ground!

So I'm going to show you how to reconnect with your social side once you've carried out the grounding technique, and also how to keep the feelings of earth safety with you. This technique is designed to be carried out immediately after 'Courage from the Earth', so when you practise 'Courage from the Earth' be sure to practise this technique too. Read all the instructions once before attempting this exercise:

1. Look at the ceiling or the sky, keeping your feet firmly planted on the ground. Then take a deep breath and slowly move your gaze downwards until you're looking straight ahead. Don't let your chin dip down – make sure it's tilted up slightly and your shoulders are thrown back.

2. Now take another deep breath and stretch your arms into the air, letting them immediately fall back down to your sides. Do this a few times until you feel lighter and your chest feels full of air.

3. Wriggle your fingers to feel the air around you and let yourself really experience breathing in and out, noting the taste and lightness of the air.

4. Take a few steps forward, continuing to look straight ahead, noting that as your feet hit the ground you still experience a strong connection to the earth from your neck downwards. But don't look down. Keep your head held high and your arms light by your sides.

5. Say either to yourself or out loud: '*I'm looking forward to a great experience and will be light, fun and sociable.*'

This releasing exercise will connect you with your fun, sociable self but it also allows you to remain safely connected to the ground and all the feelings of security that rise up from the earth.

Three-Minute Psychic Confidence

If you don't have much time before a date, or you bump into someone you like unexpectedly and need to make yourself feel calm, here is a great technique for very quickly making yourself feel relaxed, happy and confident.

You'll need a personal item, something that belongs to you that you either wear or carry around. Ideally, choose a piece of jewellery, but equally you could use a coin, book or even a hair grip. Read this technique through once before attempting it:

1. Sit down, put the personal item in your open hands and really stare at it for a few minutes – two minutes or more if you can manage it.

2. Notice your thoughts whilst you're doing this and how the object feels. Does it feel warm or cold? Does it make you feel any strong emotions?

3. After a few minutes, you'll notice you start feeling relaxed and even slightly tired. The personal object is giving you calm feelings and connecting you to your higher self.

You can use this technique in all sorts of situations, but it works particularly well where romance is concerned as it quickly calms those emotions related to love and the heart.

14

Tuning Into Your Great Date Energy

You've just learned some powerful 'grounding' techniques that put you in a calm, happy frame of mind before a date. Now you're going to use your psychic abilities to feel absolutely great about yourself and visualize a really enjoyable and fun date. I'm also going to help you understand the power of (sometimes) walking away from a situation if the psychic alarm bells are ringing, and show you how to tune into your intuition whilst you're out on a date.

Discovering Your Amazing Romantic Self

When you go on a date, it's vital you feel good about yourself and give out positive energy. Many of my clients come to me because they're not feeling great about themselves, and if you've been dating for years and have experienced lots of rejections or bad treatment, it's easy to think that perhaps you're not all that much of a catch. But you're wrong. You're a fantastic person with many unique qualities that make you a wonderful partner.

We're going to use your intuition to discover what is amazing and unique about you. Once you're brimming with the positive knowledge of your great qualities, your date won't be able to help but see the very best in you. This doesn't mean that you're trying to make every date from now on fall head over heels in love with you, or create a false image of yourself – remember, you want to find the *right* man for you, not just any man. But it does mean you'll have a better energy when you're on dates, so you'll have more fun and be more relaxed. And when you do meet the person who is perfect for you (and, yes – it will happen) you'll be showing off exactly the qualities that will make you very lovable to them.

I'd like you now to ask your intuition about your three best romantic qualities – what are the qualities that mean you're a great person to be in a relationship with? Ask your intuition:

What three things make me lovable?

Don't think, just let the answers come. What are the three best things you'll bring to a relationship? Here are some of the romantic qualities clients have told me about themselves during our sessions:

- I really care about people
- I'm funny and like to laugh
- I like to try new things and get very excited by life
- I have lots of friends and like being around people
- I'm very affectionate and loving
- I'm loyal and would never cheat on my partner

If you can't think of three qualities straight away, keep trying. Ask your intuition for more help and be patient.

> *In the eyes of the right man, your best qualities are often what you believe to be your worst qualities.*

I'd now like you to find two more positive things about yourself so you'll have five in total. But this time, instead of searching for positives, I'd like you to think of some of the qualities you like least about yourself. You're going to ask your intuition for two 'negative' qualities, because actually some of the things you don't like about yourself can be your greatest assets in the eyes of others.

1. What don't you like about yourself? 2. What do you feel doesn't appeal to other people? 3. Do you feel you're shy, self-conscious, opinionated, fussy or untidy? Believe it or not, these are great qualities if you ask your intuition to help you see them in the right way.

Let me explain. You may feel your shyness is embarrassing and unattractive, but the right person may well see you as a good listener and find your stillness rather fascinating. Perhaps you don't have lots of academic qualifications and feel people don't respect your intelligence, but actually your perfect partner will like the fact you're straightforward and easy to talk to. If you don't like your physical appearance, the chances are you don't use your looks to take advantage of other people and you're sensitive to people's feelings. These are great qualities.

Sit in a quiet place and let yourself think of two things you don't like about yourself. Now ask your intuition:

How can I see this quality in a positive, lovable way?

Be patient and let your intuition tell you the answer. Perhaps you'll discover that your 'boringness' means you're reliable, your 'chatterbox' side means you're easy to talk to and your 'flightiness' makes you exciting. Whatever your two new qualities are, I'd like you to add them to the three qualities you've just thought of. So now you have five.

Say your five romantic qualities to yourself inside your head during your date, and you'll find that positive energy spills out into the psychic aura surrounding you. Without you having to say a word, your date will 'hear' all your qualities and you'll feel much more confident and happy.

Using Great Energy to Walk Away

When you're feeling great about yourself, you'll find your confidence levels shoot up. The more you practise saying your qualities in your head, the stronger your confidence will get until it's positively shining out of you and everyone can read it in your aura. This means better dates, more respect and more fun. But it also means more *self*-respect and this is important.

When you're dating, your intuition wants to protect you. There are lots of things that can damage your self-esteem and confidence in the world of dating and romance, and your intuition wants to keep you safe. But as I've told you before, there's no point tuning into your intuition if you don't act on it. I want you to feel good about yourself so you'll have fun and attract the right partner, but also so you'll be strong enough to walk away from a date if things aren't going well. If several psychic alarm bells start ringing, and your night out is nothing like the dream date scenario you pictured for yourself (more like a dating nightmare), I want you to walk away. Politely cut the date short, go home and have faith in your intuition because it's just steered you away from a 'Mr Wrong'.

If you hang around too long with the wrong date, this can stimulate negative feelings that block your intuition and also sabotage your relationship with your psychic self. After all, your intuition is ringing psychic alarm bells in the hope that you'll listen, and if you don't act as a result of them then the chances are they'll stop ringing so loudly. Walking away from a date when your psychic alarm bells are ringing gives your psychic self and your confidence a tremendous boost, and saves your good energy for the next date.

Helen's Dating Disasters

Helen, a lovely, softly-spoken Irish lady, came to me after a disastrous date with a man called Steve. She'd met Steve at a work event and agreed to meet up with him in a bar the next night. She felt a little uneasy when Steve called her to confirm the date – although she didn't know why.

However, after a failed relationship Helen wasn't thinking all that much of herself and felt pretty lucky to be going on a date. So she ignored this psychic alarm bell and went to meet Steve at the bar as promised.

Steve turned up half an hour late, which made Helen feel unsettled – especially when he proceeded to talk at length about how overworked he was and what an awful boss he had. After an hour, he hadn't asked Helen a single question about herself, but Helen, being a relaxed and gentle soul, decided to ignore the bad feeling this gave her. 'He's probably just tired,' she thought. 'I'll give him a chance.'

Out of politeness, Helen laughed and tried to make light of the fact Steve was talking only about himself, but inside she felt very hurt and upset. The evening went from bad to worse, with Steve bumping into some friends and totally ignoring Helen.

When the date was finally over, Steve didn't even bother making sure Helen got home safely and she felt angry, upset and humiliated. The next day she discovered through work colleagues that Steve was already in a relationship, and he was late because his partner hadn't wanted him to go out to the pub again.

Helen and I worked on building up positive feelings and also on visualizing her perfect dating scenario.

Helen told me that even when she'd first met Steve at the work event, something hadn't felt quite right. This was her first psychic alarm bell and she should have been on red alert for any problems during the date. The second and third waves of uneasy feelings should have told her loud and clear: 'Get your coat and leave.'

Together, Helen and I worked on building up positive feelings and also on visualizing her perfect dating scenario. She began to feel good about herself and went on some enjoyable dates with some lovely men. However, as she continued dating she also went on another disastrous date, but this time she handled things a little differently.

Helen met date disaster number two in a bar, and he stared at her all night before coming over and asking for her number. The man's name was Bill, and they arranged to meet in the same bar the next night. But although Bill was good-looking and seemingly confident, Helen got a slightly creepy feeling from him.

The next night, when the two of them met again, Helen was on red alert. She noticed a woman in the corner of the bar staring at the pair of them during the evening, and she noticed that the barmaid seemed to be glaring at Bill. She also noticed Bill's gaze following other women around the room. After half an hour or so, Helen thanked Bill for his time and told him politely that she had to get going, at which point Bill reacted like a spoiled child who hadn't got what he wanted and tried to insist that she stay. But Helen politely refused.

A few days later, Helen found out from the barmaid that Bill had worked his magic on every woman in the local area and, in fact, as soon as Helen had gone, he'd found another lady to try his charm on.

Helen left that date with her dignity and confidence intact. She felt empowered, not humiliated, and went on to date another day.

Creating the Perfect Date

In Chapter 12, you used creative clairvoyance to see your soulmate. Now I'd like you to use creative clairvoyance again, but this time to see what a great time you're going to have on any date you go on from now on. To do this, we're going to use a great psychic technique called 'Psychic Words' to get a positive picture of what's going to happen on your date.

I'm going to ask you two questions about your dream date scenario, and I want you to look at the muddle of positive words below the questions and focus on anything that jumps out at you. You'll find the right words have a 'glow' about them. So find a comfortable, quiet spot and allow intuitive feelings to come. You might be surprised by what your intuition comes up with, but remember – your higher self knows you best.

What will happen when you meet your date?
attraction · pleasure · happiness · thoughtfulness
chivalry · romance · punctuality · gifts · compliments
smiles · physical affection · warmth · joy · delight

What will happen on your date?
flirting · laughter · fun · meeting of the minds
a new friend · a spiritual connection · enjoyment
great conversation · romance · a wonderful new experience · love · happiness · compliments · positive feelings

The purpose of this exercise is to build positive associations in your mind, so your creative clairvoyance can start building a happy picture of the future. Now you have some positive feelings about your date, I'd like you to let your mind take you on that date – and remember that it's going to be perfect. Imagine arriving at the venue, your date behaving perfectly, having a great time, really connecting with the person you're seeing and then the date ending exactly as you'd like it to.

The more you use your mind to build a positive picture of your date, the more you'll project your dream date scenario into a real-life future for youself.

Psychic Messages on a Date

Tuning into your psychic self whilst you're out on a date is important because there are many messages your intuition will want to communicate, especially if you don't know your love interest very well. But often, the date night (or day) itself is when we stop listening to our intuition. There are so many things going on – new surroundings, first-date nerves, the need to make conversation – that we forget to feel calm and tune in.

So how do you make sure, when you're out at a restaurant, cinema or other dating venue, that you're allowing psychic messages to come through? Well, just like when you've tuned into your intuition before, deep breathing is very important. I recommend that just before you meet your date you take three deep breaths in and out, counting very quickly to twenty on both the inhale and exhale. Try it now. Breathe in, counting very quickly to twenty. And breathe out, counting very quickly to twenty. You'll find this will slow your breathing and calm you down immensely. Whilst you're on the date itself, try to remember to breathe right down to your abdomen and you'll carry this calmness with you. Deep breaths cleanse the mind and make way for intuition.

Because you're out and about in public and probably chatting away, you often won't be able to clear your mind and 'hear' messages in the usual way whilst you're on a date. But as long as you're calm, your psychic self will communicate with you. How? Through your feelings.

Most people have a few nerves when they're dating, especially if they're really interested in someone, and this is fine.

When you're on a date, focus on your heart chakra, the spot in the centre of your chest just a few inches below your collarbone, and really let yourself feel the emotional messages trying to get through. If you're relaxed enough, focusing on your heart chakra will help you zoom in on your feelings and bring emotions to the surface straight away. If you're a little nervous, the messages may take a little longer, but I promise they will come through.

Feelings are the messengers of the intuition, and I'd like you to pay close attention to how you feel when you're spending time with a potential new love interest. In particular, pay close attention to how you feel when you first see your date. Most people have a few nerves when they're dating, especially if they're really interested in someone, and this is fine. But do you feel anything else? Happiness? Comfort or discomfort? Unusual levels of anxiety? Pay close attention. The amount of times I've had clients tell me 'I *knew* there was something wrong the first time I met him' is unbelievable. But so many of us ignore these feelings. Don't. Equally, don't ignore the good feelings. If you feel unusually happy and calm with your date, this is an excellent sign.

Remember — the more you practise using your intuition, the more fun and positive dating will be. You'll feel truly excited about meeting new love matches, give out a great psychic energy and really enjoy yourself. There will be some mismatches along the way — that's life, after all — but you'll still have a great time meeting new friends and soon enough your soulmate will come along.

15

Listening For Psychic Alarm Bells

Dating is great fun, and I promise you there are many nice men out there looking for loving, committed relationships. But you may also bump into one or two people who aren't good relationship material and I want your intuition to be thoroughly tuned in and on the alert for men who aren't what they seem or aren't offering what you want. In my line of work, I'm contacted by lots of heartbroken, humiliated and hurt women who unfortunately didn't listen to their intuition in the early stages of dating. When you're just getting to know people, it's not all that difficult to walk away. But if you take things further with the wrong sorts of men, you can be in for a lot of pain and embarrassment and this is what I want to help you avoid. I'm going to share with you stories of my clients who didn't follow their intuition in the early dating stages and ended up in relationships with the wrong men. I'm also going to let you know the common warning signs, or 'psychic alarm bells' that I've heard over and over again when women get involved with someone who will never offer them what they need.

As I explained in Chapter 6, psychic alarm bells are those uneasy feelings you get when something isn't quite right. They are your intuition trying to talk to you and get your attention. Your job is to listen and walk away from a date if necessary.

> **Read about the three 'Mr Wrongs' in this chapter so you can learn from the lessons of others and give your intuition a head start.**

The funny thing about psychic love counselling is that I tend to hear the same stories repeated. I meet different clients, but hear about exactly the same bad relationships and these relationships could almost always have been avoided if my clients had looked for the negative signs early on. There are three 'Mr Wrongs' I'm contacted about very often – married men, game players and those who are not ready to settle down. Whenever clients contact me about these sorts of men, I always know it's extra important to build up their own intuitive abilities so they can avoid these relationships in future. I also always point out to them the intuitive signals they missed in the beginning, so they can understand that their higher self was trying to keep them safe all along.

Perhaps you've have relationships with a few 'Mr Wrongs' yourself and want to know how to avoid them, or maybe you're new to the dating game and want to protect yourself from the wrong sorts of men. Either way, I'd recommend you read about the three 'Mr Wrongs' in this chapter so you can learn from the lessons of others and give your intuition a head start. As long as you recognize a 'Mr Wrong' early on in the dating game, you can walk away without any heartache or wasted time, and keep yourself available for 'Mr Right'.

'Mr Wrong' Number 1: The Married Man

I'm always amazed by the number of people I counsel who are in emotional hot water because they're dating a married man. Even more surprising are the amounts of clients who date married men knowing full well they are married, in the misguided hope that their man will leave his wife one day. If you're one of these ladies, let me enlighten you: in decades of psychic counselling I have *never* known a married man to leave his wife voluntarily for a mistress. There are unusual circumstances, some of which very funny, others quite tragic. But, by and large, if he was married when you started seeing him, he'll still be married when your relationship ends. And believe me – your relationship *will* end, one way or another. So spare yourself more wasted time with someone who will never offer you a full-time relationship and get out now.

But what if you're dating a married man without realizing it? I'm often contacted by clients who really had no idea their date was married, and had to endure the embarrassment and humiliation of a part-time relationship for several months before they discovered their date's secret. How do you discover he's married before things get too serious, and walk away with your pride intact?

Penelope's Married Man

Penelope was dating a man called John when she came to me for advice. She liked John a lot – he was fun, they were having a fantastic sexual relationship and he was very relaxed and comfortable in her presence. However, she was worried that something was missing. The relationship didn't really seem to be going anywhere and she saw John rarely and always on his terms. They'd meet up around once or twice a month, always at a place of John's choosing, and he seemed reluctant to share any details of his life with her. He wouldn't talk about his home life and only barely spoke of the work he did. He was, however, very attentive to Penelope and asked lots about her life and her likes and dislikes.

Penelope told me that if she could only see John more often they really would have a perfect relationship, as they were very sexually compatible and she felt they were good friends.

When I did a psychic reading for Penelope I got a strong sense that there was deception going on and that there was another woman somewhere on the scene. I asked Penelope if she'd ever felt anything untoward in John's behaviour and she told me that sometimes she felt suspicious because he never answered his phone. 'He'll always call me back ten minutes later,' Penelope explained, 'but he never picks up the phone directly. It's like he's screening the call or something. It did make me feel uneasy at first – I don't know why. I've got used to it now.' This was a very loud psychic alarm bell that Penelope should have listened to at the beginning of her relationship with John.

I asked Penelope if John had ever given her his home number, and I wasn't at all surprised when she told me he hadn't, and in fact she'd never been to his home. She and John always met at her place as John claimed his house was 'a tip' and not a great place to meet. Again, Penelope had felt uneasy about this during the early days of their relationship, but she ignored this second psychic alarm bell.

I asked Penelope to try and find out more about John when they next met – for example, where he worked. She did just that, and turned up at his workplace a few days after their meeting to surprise him. Imagine *her* surprise when the receptionist told her no one called John worked at that company!

Penelope confronted John about this, but he was very casual, saying, 'Oh, the receptionist knows me. She was probably just having an off day.' Unconvinced, Penelope asked a friend to follow John in to work one day and learned he ran a business with, you've guessed it, his wife.

Penelope visited John's company during working hours and he nearly collapsed in shock when he saw her. He told everyone at the workplace that he had no idea who Penelope was and that she was clearly insane, but Penelope was able to give personal details about John that convinced everyone that she was telling the truth.

She walked out with her head held high, but she still felt badly hurt and there was a gap in her life where John had been for several months afterwards. If only she'd listened to her intuition sooner.

Psychic Alarm Bells

What are the signs that you might be dating a married man?

- He doesn't see you very often – certainly no more than once a week, and probably more like once a month.

- He doesn't answer his phone when you call (or asks you not to call him at all) and won't give out his home number.

- He pays for everything in cash.

- He seems uneasy when you ask him about his life.

- You never see him at the weekend.

- He gives unusual answers to very basic questions about his life, or changes the subject.

How Do You Know If He's Married?

The good news about married men is that they're very easy to spot if you're in touch with your intuition. In fact, you'll probably get some uneasy feelings even before you meet up as chances are this man will be very particular about the time and place of your meeting. There's nothing wrong with being particular, of course, but if you feel uneasy inside about it, like something isn't quite right, this is a sign from your psychic side that you need to be on red alert.

Of course, there are all the classic signs to look out for with married men such as a white band where a wedding ring should be, odd behaviour with his telephone and so on. But really the easiest way to spot if someone is married or already in a relationship is to watch his body language when he talks and listen to your intuition as you watch. Do you feel he's trying to deceive you? Is something just not right? Married men give out a whole range of deception signals that any intuitive person can pick up on easily. No matter how well-practised a liar someone is, their psychic aura will always tell you the true story, so let your senses listen to the energy surrounding your date.

This is not to say you should assume that all the dates you meet might be married or in serious relationships. There really are lots of great men out there. But by being aware that the occasional 'Mr Wrong' is married or already committed, you'll let your intuition work its magic and protect yourself from a painful relationship with the wrong man.

'Mr Wrong' Number 2: The Game Player

We love bad boys, don't we? Come on, be honest, we love them – the game players who have a different girlfriend every week, talk constantly about themselves and come with big warnings from all your friends and even his friends. These men ooze sex appeal and charm and there's always that little part of us that deep down believes we'll be the one to change them. *He hasn't found the right woman so far*, we think, *but with me it's different. I'll be the one he falls madly in love with.*

But a game player is really only interested in what he can get out of you, and he is quite happy to leave you broken-hearted, lonely or clinging to the hope of a relationship for years on end so long as he gets what he wants.

Let me tell you right now, you don't want a bad boy. You want a nice man. Sometimes game players do change and mature and eventually commit to serious relationships. But any man who is still in game-playing mode won't give you the relationship you want, no matter how much care and attention you give him. So don't believe his sob story about all the awful women he dated before you. This man is egotistical and the only person he really cares about is himself.

But how do you spot a game player early on, before you're bowled over by his charm and start believing all his lies and apologies?

How Gemma Lost One-Nil

Gemma worked as a trader in the city when she came to me for love counselling. Her dream was to meet another city professional who shared her passion for hard work, and for several years she'd had her eye on a fellow trader called James. James was well-known around the office as a ladies' man and had been romantically linked to many of Gemma's colleagues, none of whom had a good word to say about him. But Gemma was sure that there was a connection between the two of them. James was always flirting with her and making excuses to touch her in some way, and Gemma could feel a real sexual chemistry between them.

On one Friday night out with work colleagues, James seemed a little down and Gemma went over to talk with him. He explained that his last girlfriend, Lisa, had cheated on him and ended their relationship and he was really devastated. He told Gemma he'd never really believed she and Lisa were all that serious, but he was hurt that she could see someone else behind his back.

Gemma was flattered that James had confided in her, and they spent several hours together during which James told Gemma about his troubled background and heroic 'rags to riches' rise to his current occupation. Gemma thought James was much more sensitive than people gave him credit for, and perhaps the women before hadn't understood what a lost little boy he was deep down.

I felt especially bad for Gemma as I could see that James had really got under her skin.

Gemma was, of course, hooked and a night of passion followed, during which James was very intense and loving. He didn't call Gemma that next week, despite promising he would, but when they met again after work the following Friday, they ended up talking again and spending another night together.

James kept telling Gemma to stay away from him, saying he was no good for her, but this would be followed by passionate nights together during which he'd tell her he loved her and had never met anyone like her before. Sometimes he'd phone late on a Saturday night and ask to meet up at Gemma's place, but he'd only ever stay for an hour or so and leave before dawn.

Two months after they'd started sleeping together, James got back together with his ex and told Gemma he couldn't see her any more. He apologized profusely and told Gemma what a fool he was and how he knew things wouldn't last with Lisa, but he was a mess and needed to sort his life out before he could be with someone as wonderful as Gemma.

When Gemma contacted me she was clearly still very much into James. His magic was still working on her, despite all the evidence that he was a game player. She was convinced that if she waited long enough he would split up with Lisa and come back to her, and they would settle into a wonderful relationship. I told her James might well come back to her, but not for a serious relationship. I felt especially bad for Gemma as I could see that James had really got under her skin and had her believing they might be a true love match; of course, his actions proved anything but.

Psychic Alarm Bells

What are the signs that you might be dating a game player?

- He talks a lot about himself, particularly the hard time he's had in life.

- He doesn't call when he says he will, but turns up in your life as and when he pleases.

- There are lots of women he's had relationships with, and he may even have many children by many different women.

- He doesn't have any female friends he hasn't slept with.

- He wants the sexual side of things to happen very quickly, before you've even really got to know each other.

- He is charming and says things that make you feel great, but his actions say he couldn't care less.

How Do You Know If He's a Game Player?

Game players have just one thing on their mind – themselves. The trouble is that in order to get their own way, game players often have very clever and devious tactics for making it *look* like they care about you and have your best interests at heart. They may tell you how beautiful you are and how you've changed their life, but if they're not returning your calls or breaking down doors to see you, the chances are they're not interested in a serious relationship.

The key to spotting game players is to pay attention to their actions, *not* their words. If he's full of apologies and excuses for being late but is *always* late, pay attention to the action. Lateness shows lack of respect. Your intuition really is your best friend when it comes to spotting game players because when you're out of touch with your psychic energy you tend to put great importance on the words people say. But with your intuition working for you, you'll sense the whole picture. Someone who cares about you puts your interests first. Is this what your date is doing?

> *If he was genuinely interested in getting to know you, there'd be no hurry to move the sex side of things along.*

Another thing I notice when my clients date game players is that the sex side of things moves very quickly. He may offer all sorts of wonderful compliments about how beautiful you are and how he's never met a woman like you, but the truth is he doesn't know all that much about you. If he was genuinely interested in getting to know you, then there'd be no hurry to move the sex side of things along.

Game players work on the basis that women love lots of attention and compliments — so much so that women often believe everything they're told by someone who compliments them and they ignore that little voice in their head that says: *Hang on a minute, this is all a bit too good to be true*. And this, of course, gives the game player the opportunity to get exactly what he wants, be it sex, money, a place to stay, an ego boost or something else.

Because you're going to pay attention to your intuition from now on, you're not going to be the sort of woman who hears only the words your date says. You'll be calm and able to read his psychic aura and be on the alert for the uncomfortable feelings that tell you his words don't match his actions.

'Mr Wrong' Number 3: The Commitment-Phobe

Are you dating a man who is scared of commitment? There are some men out there who are quite simply terrified of settling down. They may have vague ideas of marriage and a family in the future, the very distant future, but for now committing to one woman scares the life out of them.

The interesting thing about commitment-phobes is that they often date very beautiful, successful and talented women, the sorts of women that every other man wants to date, but this doesn't seem to make any difference to their commitment issues. It's not a question of finding the right woman to commit to. For commitment-phobes, as soon as any woman mentions 'long term', they go running in the opposite direction.

Men who are scared of commitment can be difficult to spot in the early stages of dating, and this is what makes them so dangerous. It isn't until you've got in too deep that you begin to realize the man you're seeing simply won't commit to a proper, adult relationship. But there are definitely clear signs if you know what to look for, and I'm going to help you see them.

Jennifer's Commitment-Phobic Man

Jennifer, a lovely 35-year-old, was full of life and happiness when she first came to me for relationship advice. But she'd had a run of bad luck when it came to dating and was having problems in her latest relationship with a man called Dale. She and Dale had been stuck in a rut for over a year and didn't seem to be moving forward.

When I asked Jennifer about the early days of their relationship, the thing she remembered most clearly was that she'd felt a sense of chasing after Dale, even though she'd been careful not to phone him too often and had let him do all the asking out. Also, Dale hadn't been too happy about the idea of paying for all their dates together so Jennifer had obligingly stumped up for half their meals out and cinema visits in order for everything to be fair. Although Jennifer had felt a little uncomfortable about this, she acknowledged that in modern times it was only reasonable for women to pay their way. However, it didn't make her feel very feminine or special.

As the months went by, Jennifer and Dale had fun together but everything always seemed to be on Dale's terms and any schedule suggested by Jennifer was either rearranged or cancelled. Dale lived quite a way away from Jennifer and had a full-time job, so although Jennifer felt bad inside whenever a date was cancelled or rearranged, she put it down to the fact there was such a distance between them and that Dale was busy.

If Jennifer hung around for five years, or even ten years, there would be no guarantee that Dale would want to move things forward.

After a year of dating, the couple still went on dates every week and saw each other regularly, but their relationship hadn't moved forward and Dale was in no rush to change things. Jennifer had tentatively suggested moving in together, but for Dale there were always practical reasons why this couldn't happen – his house was too small for both of them and he couldn't sell it right now, and he couldn't move in with Jennifer because he'd be too far away from work.

When Jennifer suggested having children in the next few years, Dale reacted very badly and told her he had far too much to sort out at work before this could ever happen. He told her maybe in five years this could be a possibility, but certainly not before.

Jennifer was beginning to realize what to me was obvious: Dale was scared of commitment and even if Jennifer hung around for five years, or even ten years, there would be no guarantee that Dale would want to move things forward. At the moment, he was having his cake and eating it. He had a casual relationship that gave him everything he needed, but required barely any commitment from him. Jennifer let him come and go as he pleased, arrange and cancel dates as he pleased and generally be free as a bird, whilst she sat around waiting for him to decide to get serious.

Psychic Alarm Bells

What are the signs that you might be dating a commitment-phobe?

- He's had many short-term relationships but never been married.

- He's happy to have a long-distance relationship.

- Dating isn't his first priority – it comes a poor second to his job, his friends and his possessions.

- He's looking specifically for independent business-women with lives of their own.

- He's changed careers many times and has a job that gives him a lot of freedom.

- He doesn't like routine and often cancels or reschedules dates.

How Do You Know He's a Commitment-Phobe?

As I said previously, commitment-phobes can be very difficult to spot in the early stages of dating, but there are big signs if you know where to look. The main thing my clients tell me they feel in the early stages of dating a commitment-phobe is that they are doing the chasing, rather than the other way round. One way or another, they're always the ones waiting around outside the restaurant or phoning him to ask where he is or just generally feeling

228

like he isn't all that bothered about the date at all. That's because he isn't. After all, he's got nothing to lose. He's not interested in a long-term relationship, so it makes little difference to him how happy you are.

The other thing clients almost always mention about commitment-phobic people is that they're generally quite irresponsible. They may work, but it's usually a casual arrangement and they can come and go as they please. Often they're self-employed. They may have a house, but they don't maintain it particularly well, or they pay other people to maintain and clean it for them. They're unlikely to have any hobbies that require a great deal of work and they prefer renting to buying outright.

More than with any other type of date, you need to be closely in touch with your psychic energy to spot a commitment-phobe because it is your feelings, not logic, that will tell you this person is no good in the long term. Commitment-phobes are a dangerous breed who can be very bad for your self-esteem, but with your intuition helping you I promise you can read the warning signs early on, move on and find someone who is only too happy to have a serious, long-term relationship with you.

PART V

Using Intuition When You Begin a Relationship

16

Are We in Psychic Harmony?

It's exciting to begin a relationship, especially if you've been dating or been single for a long time. But the start of a romance is not the time to abandon your intuition. On the contrary – you need your psychic powers more than ever because passion and excitement can chatter over your psychic mind and dull your ability to hear when something isn't right.

This is not to say you should be pessimistic when you start a relationship, but it's true when they say love is blind. The excitement of romance and infatuation can temporarily close your 'third eye' to the true nature of your love match and the chances of long-term compatibility.

If you've been on lots of dates with your new romantic match, hopefully you'll have already tuned into your intuition and listened for any psychic alarm bells. But how can you be sure, once you've decided that your date is worth getting to know better, that the two of you are on the same wavelength and well-tuned to each other in the long term?

In the next chapter, we'll look at common questions clients ask me when they're beginning a new relationship. These questions are:

Is he ready for commitment?
Does he genuinely care about me?
Are we compatible?
Will he bring out the best in me?

But before we do that, I'd like to show you how to check-in with your psychic energy levels to discover how your relationship is making you feel so far. I'm going to show you how to tune into your aura and use colours to understand how beneficial this new relationship is to your wellbeing.

Reading Your Psychic Energy

Your aura is the psychic energy surrounding you, the invisible glow you give out that can be sensed by others. Many psychics 'see' auras as colours surrounding the body, and they 'read' these colours as different moods and qualities affecting the person at that time. A psychic aura reader can also see if there are any coloured energy blockages around your body and understand whether you need to work on nervous or negative energy.

Just like everyone has psychic abilities, so everyone can read auras. Reading other people's auras as colours takes a lot of practice, but reading your own aura is quite straight forward and I'm going to show you how to do it. Practising aura reading is also a great way to strengthen your intuition and the more you let yourself 'see' auras, the easier it will be to read colours around other people as well as yourself.

When you get a sense of the colours around your body and what these mean for your energy and mood, you'll understand more about your current relationship and how well you and your partner are harmonizing on a psychic level. Because your aura is always changing, sometimes even from day to day, reading your colours will give you an excellent sense of what your current partner brings out of you and the psychic energy you are building together.

Most aura readers see the psychic energy that surrounds people as a colour, and I'm going to teach you about the basic aura colours and what they mean about energy and mood. When you think of the colour red, what do you feel? Energized? Excited? What about the colour blue? Do you find it calming? If I asked you to paint your bedroom a very bright yellow colour, how would you feel about that? What if you walked into a hospital and the walls were painted black or grey?

Our intuition has powerful links with colour. In fact, the relationship between our psychic side and colour is so strong that everyone has feelings about certain colours that defy logical explanation.

Of course, in the world we live in today, where colours are used by advertisers to try and stimulate our senses and memory, be aware that some of your intuitive feelings can get confused. You might, for example, think of the red of a fast-food logo or the green of a petrol station and wrongly associate these colours with products or commercials. But there will always be a stock of colours you have feelings about, which I hope shows you how firmly colours are linked to your intuitive understanding.

Reading Your Romantic Aura

I'm now going to show you how to read your own aura, but you're going to do more than just a general aura reading. You're going to read the aura that relates to your emotional life and your new partner. This means you'll be reading the psychic energy that your partner brings out of you.

You'll need a quiet room and a full-length mirror. Sit down on the floor or on a chair in front of the mirror and breathe deeply, closing your eyes and clearing your mind of conscious thought. Make sure the room is nice and light and that daylight is visible if possible. You may want to play some soothing music if you find this helps you, or light some candles or incense.

As you breathe deeply, think of your partner. Perhaps remember recent time spent together or think of a gift he has bought you or an item of clothing you associate with him. Put your hand to your chest a few inches below your collar bone (this is your heart chakra), and feel love energy flowing into this spot.

After a few minutes of deep breathing, open your eyes and look softly at your reflection in the mirror. What colours do you see and where are they? You may see perhaps a rich purple covering your whole body, flashes of yellow around your head and green around your heart. Perhaps there is a silver colour swirling around your hands and patches of blue near your feet. Let the colours come. You may hear names of colours rather than see them floating around your body, and this is fine.

You're reading your energy, qualities and feelings as they relate to your partner right now, but remember your colours can change over time. Now let's look at the colours you sensed around your body, and what they mean for love and energy compatibility.

Love Colours

Gold: You have a very good understanding of your body and your energy level is high. Your mood is upbeat and you have excellent levels of awareness. Your partner is good for your soul and nourishes your spirit.

True Yellow: You are happy, quick-thinking and able to learn fast. You're great fun to be around and your mood is playful. You have lots of drive and enthusiasm but can be a little critical of others. Your partner stimulates you, makes you feel lively and helps you think clearly.

Pale Yellow: You like being alone right now and feel a little vulnerable around other people. This suggests that your partner is perhaps not nurturing you as much as you would like, or that you're facing new challenges in your romantic life. Be honest with your partner, tell him your fears and ask for his support.

Lemon Yellow: You're strong and dynamic and aren't letting anyone get in your way. Your partner boosts this strength and supercharges you, making you feel you can accomplish anything.

Gold Yellow: You're bright, alert and capable and do everything thoroughly and carefully. You are well-balanced and have plenty of energy. Your partner keeps you emotionally stable and boosts your good feelings about yourself.

Green: You're emotionally stable and at ease, and feel very secure at present. You want to grow and learn and your partner really helps you do this, showing you a whole other side to life and helping you develop in healthy ways.

Dark Green: This is the colour of stress and overwork. You feel you've taken on too much, but aren't sure how to ask for help. Your partner may be just too much for you to handle, and isn't contributing to a good state of mind. Talk to him about your feelings and see if your energy changes.

Orange: You're creative and artistic and able to express yourself freely. You're happy, in good health and enjoying life. Your partner helps bring out your creative and fun side, but you need to talk about stability and shared goals for the future in order to put your relationship on a firm path.

Red: You have a real passion for life and a strong sense of self, but you're also feeling angry and frustrated. Your partner is holding you back in some way or not communicating properly. You need to decide if this situation is resolvable or if the two of you are too mismatched to work in the long term.

Brown: You're grounded and practical and aren't too keen on change. Your partner keeps you firmly rooted and offers a simple, easy-going life together. Is this what you're looking for? If it is – fine. But if you secretly feel you're more suited to something more exciting, it's time to rethink your relationship.

Very Dark Brown: You're hard-working and are well-connected with common sense and practical things. Your partner makes you feel sensible and perhaps even staid at times, but appreciates the stability you offer and advice you give.

Black/Dark Grey: Something is missing at the moment and you probably feel a little depressed. Black or dark grey colours suggest energy blocks, so you're most likely feeling trapped, fearful or nervous and that you're missing out on something. Seeing these colours suggests your partner is stifling your spiritual development and blocking you in some way. Your partner may also have a problem with addictions or be stimulating the addictive side of your character.

Blue: You're good at communicating with others and love feeling organized and neat. Your energy at this time is more male than female, and you want to take things safely and slowly, dealing with situations as calmly as possible. There is a touch of loneliness to this colour, suggesting you're not connecting with your partner as closely as you could and that you're very much operating as two individuals rather than a couple. But there is also a feeling of calm, happiness and balance that suggests a stable match.

Light Blue: You're sensitive and very in touch with your intuitive senses. Your partner respects your feelings and lets you be yourself. You can be open and honest around your partner and he in turn is completely himself around you.

Aqua: You're very in touch with healing powers and make others feel calm and well. Your partner makes you feel good, but may be something of a 'rescue' project. Do you nurture him and quietly take the credit for his improvement? Make sure the nurturing works both ways.

Turquoise: You're dynamic and successful and really

moving forward in life. Your partner is happy for you to do well and the two of you support each other intellectually and emotionally.

Purple: You're a very wise soul and highly intuitive, with a strong personality that means you like to be in charge. You love being around people and tuning into your spiritual side. Your partner respects you, your strength and your spirituality, but make sure you're not too domineering in the relationship.

Soft Pink: You're feeling a lot of love right now, both towards yourself and others. This is a very female energy, which suggests your partner brings out your passive, softer side and likes to protect you and keep you safe.

Bright Pink: You work very hard and find it hard to stop and relax. Your partner adds to this feeling of pressure and your workload, perhaps by failing to meet your expectations or requests. The question is: are your expectations too high, or is your partner not giving enough?

Pearl/Cream: You're superbly tuned to your spiritual side and have many visions and insights into the future. Your partner relaxes you and makes you feel safe and comfortable.

Very Light Grey: You're working strongly on your spiritual energy, and have excellent meditative abilities. You're also well-balanced, but you're running away from something – some feeling or emotional challenge. Your partner is trying to get closer to you but you're keeping him at arm's length. Why?

Silver: This is an exciting colour that suggests you're in touch with higher guidance and receiving wise and true messages. Your partner loves and respects the real you and you're able to be both vulnerable and strong in his presence.

White (clear white): You have a very strong spiritual connection and are compassionate and clear-thinking. Your partner matches you well and helps you see life in different ways.

This is a basic overview of aura colours, but there are many shades in between and they all have various meanings. Let your intuition guide you as to the feelings you get from each colour – especially if you see colours that aren't listed here. You may find you also get different senses when you try to understand auras and energy fields. Perhaps sounds or even smells. Be patient and let your higher self unfold the meanings of these other senses.

Yasmin's Love Aura

Usually, I work as a psychic counsellor and give advice based on my sense of a situation. But from time to time, I see colours surrounding people – their aura – and this can give me a really interesting insight into their mood and energy. I remember very vividly doing a psychic reading for a lady called Yasmin, and as soon as she walked into the room I sensed a pink colour surrounding her. It wasn't easy for me to see at first – it was as if the colour was just on the edge of my vision and I needed stronger glasses. But I could definitely sense it, and I asked Yasmin if she minded me getting a feeling for her aura during the consultation.

Yasmin agreed, and as the reading went on the pink became stronger and I saw silver colours also. This suggested she was feeling very feminine and loving, and was also well connected with her own intuitive energies. She'd just entered a new relationship with a man who was quite different to the men she'd dated in the past, and the purpose of the reading was to get a sense of whether this person was right for her or not. The pink colour around her said clearly to me that this man was bringing out the best in her.

Yasmin confirmed that she was feeling more loving and feminine than she had done in years, and that the man she was seeing, a fitness instructor who she ordinarily would have dismissed as being too young, was protective and supportive and made her feel safe and loved.

Sensing Blocked Energy

I remember, whilst working with an aura-reading friend of mine, she saw a greyish light completely surrounding one of her clients and she was getting a strong feeling that this man's energy was blocked or stagnated in some way. When I talked to my aura-reading companion, she explained that the man had suffered a stroke many years before but had never truly recovered. He felt low and depressed and had almost no energy.

This is an extreme example of seeing energy blocks, but you may notice, when you begin seeing colours in your energy field, that certain areas of your body glow more freely with colour than others, or that you have a heavy black or grey energy focused on certain areas of your body. This can indicate emotional energy blockages and areas that need healing attention.

Aura readings are related to the energy chakras, which are key energy points located all over your body. Good aura readers can see colours surrounding your energy chakras, and this indicates how various parts of your body and soul are feeling, physically, emotionally and spiritually. As your psychic senses improve, you may well see colours attached to certain areas, or 'power points', on your body that relate to the energy chakras. There are seven energy chakras in total. You can see where the key energy chakras are located on the body in the diagram below.

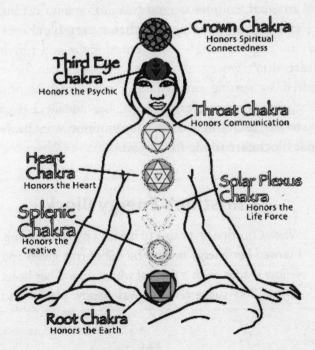

Crown Chakra
Honors Spiritual
Connectedness

Third Eye
Chakra
Honors the Psychic

Throat Chakra
Honors Communication

Heart
Chakra
Honors the Heart

Solar Plexus
Chakra
Honors the
Life Force

Splenic
Chakra
Honors the
Creative

Root Chakra
Honors the Earth

When a specific area of your body is holding a black, white or dark grey colour, this suggests an energy block and it's important to pay attention to the area where the block occurs. If you're thinking about relationships, the energy chakra you need to pay particular attention to is the one at your heart area, which is your emotional centre. However, I've known people in mismatched relationships have black or dark grey colours around their throat area (communication problems), lower abdomen (sexual incompatibility), forehead (third eye and intuition blockages) and base of the spine (problems with long-term compatibility).

Pay very close attention to energy blockages when reading your romantic aura, as they can really flag up issues and challenges that need to be addressed. If you feel any dark colours around you during aura readings, it is important to think about what energy blockages you may be experiencing – both emotionally and physically. Please don't worry, as energy blockages can be easily cleared by sorting out whatever emotional or physical imbalance you're suffering from, but equally I do want you to pay attention and ask your intuition what messages these blocks are trying to tell you.

Christine's Energy Block

When Christine first came to me for a psychic reading, I sensed her energy field to be full of true green and yellow shades, with a flash of white around her heart centre. This suggested she was happy, playful and well-balanced, with a real spirituality connected to her emotions. However, when Christine began a relationship with a very successful lawyer, I noticed a dip in her mood. I sensed her psychic energy field was filled with red, bright pink and very dark brown. Around her heart centre was a greyish, black colour which gave me real cause for concern as this suggested her emotions were being blocked in some way.

As we discussed her new relationship, it became clear to me that this emotional, child-like and spiritual woman was not meshing well with the logical and crisply intelligent lawyer she had begun a relationship with. He didn't take well to discussions about feelings or talk of spirituality, so Christine had found herself stifling her true self. As a result she was blocked, frustrated and bored, and her whole life felt like hard work now as she was struggling to change her character to fit her new partner.

Christine realized that she and the lawyer weren't right together, and as she began distancing herself from him and resuming her old hobbies, such as yoga, meditation and dance classes, I was happy to see her energy field return to its usual vibrant yellows and greens during her next consultation.

17

Is This a Long-Term Love?

How do you know that love is long term? So many clients contact me at the beginning of a relationship, when those nerve-racking first dates are out of the way and things are starting to get serious, and they are desperate to know: 'Will this love last?' After years of uncertainty and heartbreak, clients want certainty. They want to know for sure that they're not wasting their time with their current love interest, and that they won't have to endure another unpleasant relationship break-up sometime down the line.

I counsel a lot of my clients to look out for warning signs when they begin relationships, but it's just as important to know that a relationship is healthy and on the right track.

I'm going to share with you now the top four questions clients ask me when they begin a new relationship, and tell you how to spot the positive signs that suggest you've picked a genuine, caring person who will work at making your relationship last.

The questions I'm most commonly asked are:

Does he genuinely care about me?
Is he committed to me?

246

Are we compatible?
Will he bring out the best in me?

We're going to look at these questions one by one, and I'll relate to you stories of my clients who found wonderful relationships and the signs that told them they were on the right track. Rather than looking for 'psychic alarm bells', I'll share with you the 'psychic love signs' that told my clients they were heading for a healthy, loving relationship.

Long-Term Love Question 1: Does He Genuinely Care About Me?

Men who genuinely care about you put your needs before their own, and this is a recipe for a wonderful relationship. They're interested in you and what's going on in your life, they go out of their way to make you happy and they have respect for who you are. This doesn't mean they'll always remember every little detail about you and your tastes. They may say the wrong thing, buy you presents you don't like and like a bit of time to themselves now and again, but deep down their aim is your happiness.

When you find a man like this, it's time to put all your anxieties to one side and appreciate what a great person you're in a relationship with. Make sure you feel good about yourself and use positive thinking to project a good psychic aura, because if you're happy then he's happy.

Callie's Love Turnaround

For many years, a client of mine called Callie was in a relationship with a man called Oliver who cared more about himself than he cared about her. At first, the relationship had been good and he'd made an effort, but after a year together he spent more time playing computer games than he spent time with Callie. He put on weight, refused any attempts at arranging nights out, forgot Callie's birthday and gave her money to buy her own Christmas presents.

Callie began to feel depressed. Deep down, she blamed herself for the way the relationship was going because Oliver constantly accused her of nagging or being too demanding. Whenever she tried to talk to Oliver about changing things, he became angry and defensive or changed the subject, which meant Callie rarely bothered talking to him about things at all. Oliver didn't cheat on Callie or flirt with other women so she thought he must care about her – after all, he'd agreed to move into her flat and hadn't left.

When I talked to Callie I could sense she was feeling very fragile and low, and I pointed out to her that if she was in a happy relationship, she wouldn't feel this way. We did a psychic reading together and it seemed clear to me she had lots of good friends around her and should spend more time with them to boost her confidence and happiness.

Callie began seeing her friends more and more – something she'd neglected to do for a while because Oliver just wanted to sit around the house. Through these friends, she became close to a slightly older man called Tom. He wasn't her usual type, but he made her feel very loved and cared about, and he'd always make sure she got home safely and told her to text him when she arrived back so he knew she was OK.

Gradually, Callie and Tom began seeing more of each other – just as friends at first, and this was fine with Tom who was happy to get to know Callie on her terms. Callie began making more of an effort with her appearance and dressing up and Tom was hugely complimentary about how she looked, whereas Oliver didn't even notice her new outfits.

It became clear to Callie that, Tom or no Tom, things had to end with Oliver. Now she was feeling better about herself and had the attention of someone who really cared, it was obvious that Oliver actually wasn't all that fussed about her. It had got to the point where she didn't even want to come home to Oliver any more, so one day she packed her things and left, leaving a note telling Oliver that she was lonely in the relationship and wanted more.

It wasn't long before Callie and Tom got together properly, and she is now blissfully happy. Tom is still incredibly caring and attentive, just as he was in the early days of their relationship, and their love has grown and grown.

Psychic Love Signs

What are the signs that he genuinely cares about you?

- He calls, sends emails and texts you all the time.

- He always sounds delighted to hear from you.

- He chooses date venues and presents that match your tastes and personality.

- He often does things to make your life easier and happier, such as small chores around the house or picking you up after a late night at work.

- If you reach out to hold his hand, he grabs to hold yours.

- He is happy to give you his time and attention, but doesn't expect anything in return except for your happiness.

How Do You Know He Genuinely Cares About You?

Your intuition has a very special way of showing you that a man genuinely cares for you. It will make you feel warm, contented, special and safe. If your new partner is giving out lots of signs that he really cares, but you feel shaky, uneasy and paranoid, you need to take time out, do the Psychic Staircase or similar meditative exercise and ask your intuition what's really going on. Are you being paranoid and thinking about past, failed relationships? Are these feelings coming from your logical brain (*If he really loved me, he would have bought me those shoes I said I wanted . . . He smiled at my friend, so maybe that means he likes her instead . . .*) or your intuitive brain (*I can* feel *something isn't quite right . . .*)?

Deep down, when you think of your new love interest, what feelings do you get? Are they good or bad?

When my clients are in a relationship with a genuinely caring man they always seem more happy and contented, even if their logical brain is thinking about how things could go wrong. And when I ask them for their feelings about their new partner, they always say healthy things such as: 'He's very loving and kind.'

If you're feeling uneasy and you can't honestly say that you're certain your new partner has your best interests at heart, it might be time to think about the early days of your relationship and consider any warning signs you might have missed.

If, on the other hand, your feelings suggest you're in a relationship with someone who really cares about your happiness but you keep worrying about things going wrong, try reading about your powers of attraction in Chapter 5 and ask your intuition:

How can I feel more positive about myself?

Long-Term Love Question 2: Are We Compatible?

When the passion and excitement of lust at first sight have died down, many of my clients want to know if they are compatible with their new partners in the long term. This is a very sensible question. Passion is wonderful, but for a relationship to last there must also be a deep friendship and soul connection – otherwise you're left with a sexual relationship and nothing more. So how do you know if there is genuine compatibility between you and your new partner, or if you're just experiencing the closeness that comes from a great sexual bond?

Psychic energy is very important when it comes to compatibility, as it is through this energy that you know, *really* know, if you and your partner are soulmates or just sexual playmates. Your partner may have different hobbies and interests to you, but if their psychic energy blends with yours then you have long-lasting compatibility that means a lifetime of love.

Stacy's Soul Match

Some time ago, I counselled a lovely lady called Stacy who had fallen head-over-heels for an accountant called David. Stacy was a flower designer and was worried that her new man, who she'd recently moved in with, might be just too different to make a compatible match in the long term. After all, they had completely different jobs and social lives, and whilst her job was creative and artistic, his was anything but.

However, David had a deep love and respect for Stacy and her profession, and encouraged her in her creative endeavours, requesting that she place flowers around their home and decorate as she saw fit. In return, Stacy was also in awe of David and his abilities with finances.

The pair enjoyed spending time together, got on well with each other's friends and families and were always bubbling with things to say to each other at the end of the working day. In short, they were best friends, and Stacy told me she and David were '*on the same wavelength*' even on their first date.

These two people were very different, but their souls were perfectly matched. On the surface they were dissimilar, but actually their energies were very similar and complementary. How could I tell? Because Stacy was well over the honeymoon stage and still glowing with love and praise for David. Seventeen years later, Stacy and David are still happily married. They rarely argue, have no regrets or resentments and are truly happy together. Despite their differences, their souls are still best friends.

Psychic Love Signs

What are the signs that the two of you are compatible?

- You never feel tongue-tied or run out of things to say around your partner.

- The honeymoon period is over, but you still love being around each other.

- You describe yourselves as best friends, and know that, relationship or not, you'll always want to spend time together.

- When you met, you felt like you'd known your partner for years.

- You like each other's friends.

- You might like different things, but you approve of each other's choices and lifestyles.

How Do You Know if the Two of You Are Compatible?

The feeling of true compatibility isn't something that can be measured or monitored. It is simply the calm knowledge inside that the two of you are great friends and will always remain great friends, no matter what differences you have.

Of course, I have been contacted by clients who are with a wonderful, compatible partner but letting their own worries and concerns (often based on past relationships) get in the way of happiness. It's hard to tell, when your psychic aura is clouded with doubt and anxiety, if you're with a true friend or not. But my advice is this: trust yourself and your intuition. If you're letting logical thoughts such as 'But our families are totally different' or 'I know nothing about his type of work and he knows nothing about mine' get in the way, notice them for what they are – logic. Relationships are to do with feelings, both sexual feelings and emotional feelings. The important feelings for long-term compatibility are your emotional feelings – are the two of you emotionally in tune? Do you give each other the attention you both require and respond to each other in ways that make both of you happy?

Get in touch with your psychic self and state very clearly that you want to look past the passionate, sexual side of your relationship and see the true feelings underneath, as these are the feelings that will tell you if your souls are truly compatible. If you sense a deep friendship, then you know the two of you are a compatible match.

Long-Term Love Question 3: Will He Bring Out the Best in Me?

You were put on this earth to do something amazing, and your perfect partner will ensure you do just that. The right partner will bring out the very best in you, ensuring you have a great connection with your psychic energies and live up to your full potential. This means they will support you in the things that really matter in your life, and truly believe in your abilities. A partner who brings out the best in you is positive, nurturing and supportive, and helps make you the best person you can be.

You may be with a partner who shares your values and makes you feel wonderful, but how do you know they are truly helping you live up to your potential?

Daria's Business Dream

Daria was a beautician client of mine who dreamed of opening her own nail studio, offering quirky, creative nail painting among other services, in the centre of her home town. For many years, she'd been with a partner called Graham who, although a kind-hearted person, didn't believe in Daria's dreams and felt strongly that she should 'stick with what she knew' and carry on working as a beautician for an established company.

As time went on, Daria became more miserable. She began to realize that she and Graham wanted very different things – he was happy to keep their life small and contented, whereas she wanted to change and grow. Inside, Graham was quite an insecure person who didn't like change, and whilst he would have been the perfect partner for someone who wanted stability and reliability, he was holding Daria back and stopping her from living the life of her dreams.

After much soul-searching, Daria took a brave step and split with Graham, realizing that as long as they were together she would never move forward. She began looking for a rental property for her nail bar and in the process met Paul, a property consultant who was a very optimistic and confident person. The two of them struck up a relationship, during which Paul was hugely encouraging of Daria's new business venture and gave her lots of positive support and good advice.

Three years later, Daria's new nail bar was busy and profitable, and she and Paul were very much in love. She told me that now she was with a truly supportive partner, a partner who really saw her potential, she felt the sky was the limit and she could see nothing but sunshine on the horizon.

Psychic Love Signs

What are the signs that your partner brings out the best in you?

- You feel encouraged and know your partner believes in your abilities.

- Your partner is keen for you to try new things, even if there is a chance of failure.

- You never feel your partner is trying to change you or run your life.

- Your partner listens to you but doesn't give unsolicited advice.

- You know your partner trusts you to take charge of your own life.

- The two of you are completely open about your ambitions and dreams.

How Do You Know Your Partner Brings Out the Best in You?

When a partner brings out the best in you, you will feel optimistic and excited about life. You will find yourself believing in your own potential and capabilities, and feel unafraid to try new things or visit new places.

In my experience, when people are with partners who

aren't bringing out the best in them, they feel afraid to try new things and generally have a more negative mindset. Of course, a negative mindset isn't always the fault of a mismatched relationship, and we all have to take responsibility for developing a positive attitude on a daily basis. But if your intuition is telling you that your partner is holding you back and putting a negative block on your dreams, it's time to check in with your psychic self and think long and hard about your relationship. What do you really want to be and do in life? Can you imagine doing these things with your partner? Or do you feel your partner would be negative or unsupportive and ultimately keep you from living the life you want?

Sometimes I talk with clients who keep their dreams private from their partner. Deep down, they feel that if they shared these personal ambitions and wishes, they will be mocked or scorned in some way. Do you feel this to be true of your relationship? If you haven't shared your dreams with your partner, it's very important that you do so. You may be disappointed if your partner offers a negative reaction – in which case it's time to think long and hard about your relationship. But you may also be pleasantly surprised by how supportive and positive your partner is.

Often, I find people don't share their dreams because they don't want to make themselves vulnerable. But fear of vulnerability can put a real block on your relationship and leave you without the support that your partner wants to give. If you're feeling under-confident, try some of the self-esteem boosting exercises in Chapter 5. Then share your dreams with your partner. The sooner you do so, the sooner you'll know whether you're in a truly supportive relationship. And more often than not, I find that people's partners really do want to nurture and bring out the best in them.

18

Using Your Powers to Build True Love

Your psychic powers are designed to do more than simply bring you true love. Their purpose is also to help you keep hold of love, and build a nurturing, happy and exciting relationship that stands the test of time. When you're in tune with your intuition, love will grow, blossom and flower because you are truly connecting with another human being on a psychic level and experiencing a relationship of the soul. But you must still work on your psychic abilities, particularly the energy you give out, as this can help or hinder your relationship. Like attracts like, so keeping an eye on your aura and making sure it's as positive as it can be will do wonders for your love life.

It's also important, once you're in a relationship, to ensure your energies remain a little bit separate if you want love to flourish. This might sound strange. After all, aren't relationships about two people coming together? Yes, they are. But to keep love fresh and exciting, it's important for couples to work on their own lives, independently of each other, to ensure their two energies are different enough to create a healthy, complementary partnership when they meet. To do this, you must check in with your psychic side from time-to-time to remind yourself of your own unique energy and powers.

Letting Go of Perfection

As the honeymoon period begins to fade and your relationship becomes a real part of your life, so the realities of your partner hit home. Your partner isn't perfect. They have bad habits. They don't agree with you about everything and sometimes do or say things that drive you mad. Perhaps there are even things about them that make you doubt your long-term compatibility. Rest assured that all these things are usually normal and nothing to worry about. I've counselled many healthy couples over the years and they all have their various niggles and gripes with each other from time to time. If you told me your partner was perfect, I'd start worrying about you because I'd think you were keeping something from me. Small imperfections are part of any healthy relationship.

Once the rose-tinted spectacles slip and you start seeing your partner as a real person, rather than the perfect vision of love you first met, you must be very careful not to give out the negative psychic energy that can turn a great relationship sour. Seeing minor imperfections in a partner can put you in a negative, critical frame of mind, rather than a positive, loving one, and you must learn to control your psychic energy to make sure you are giving out the right kind for a good relationship.

Remember I told you that like attracts like? If your aura is negative, you'll attract negativity – both from your partner and the wider world. As I've previously explained, your aura can be read by other people and if you're feeling negatively towards your partner, they will be able to sense it. This will build negativity between the two of you as they respond to your critical energy.

> *I've found that negativity between two people comes down to one key thing: differences.*

So it's very important to take responsibility for your psychic energy when you're in a relationship and ensure this energy is as positive as it can be. This doesn't mean you can't have 'off' days or feel down from time-to-time, but it does mean you must work hard each day to create a positive energy around you and to see the best in your partner and your relationship.

So how do you make sure, once you're in a relationship, that your aura stays positive and upbeat? First, let's look at what tends to make people feel negative in a relationship. During the psychic counselling sessions I've held for people in healthy relationships, I've found that negativity between two people comes down to one key thing: differences.

You are different from your partner – that's part of what attracted you to them in the first place. You like different things, have different habits, prefer different people and TV programmes and come from different families. Of course, I'm sure there are also things about you that are similar. Your values, your attitude to life, your love for one another . . . But it is the differences that tend to make people think negatively of their partner, and project – quite unnecessarily – negative energy into their psychic aura that can turn a good relationship bad.

In order to turn negative psychic energy, the sort of energy that hates anything different and unusual, into a healthy, positive psychic energy that respects your partner and their differences, you must remember why the differences in your partner are perfect for you. Whilst you were dating, you fully realized why the wonderful differences in your partner were so good for you. Perhaps their lovely, calm temperament was captivating to your changeable spirit and made you feel safe and grounded. Maybe their fire and dynamism made you enjoy things you would never have experienced on your own.

For many people, however, once a relationship gets underway, 'perfect' behaviour in a partner really means 'behaving just like me'. If you like hanging towels up straight after you've used them, you feel a 'perfect' partner would do exactly the same thing. Perhaps you love seafood and watching romantic films. Wouldn't a 'perfect' partner like that too, so we could share this experience together? And, of course, there is also the idea society has of a 'perfect' partner – someone with money, good looks, charm, a perfect family and no emotional baggage.

But 'perfect' is not the same as 'perfect for you'. If your partner loves and respects you, and you're generally happy, then they are perfect for you. Full stop. There is nothing to be gained from dwelling on their differences in a negative way and projecting this negativity into your relationship.

You must use your psychic abilities properly and wisely, and make sure you are projecting positive energy whenever you can.

> *As long as you're feeling positive about your partner inside, you will project a healthy, happy positive energy into your psychic aura.*

So I want you to remember now why your partner's differences or 'imperfections' are good for you. Write a list of the things that are 'wrong' with your partner. What irritates you? What upsets you? What drives you mad? The list can be as long as you like.

Now for each of these 'wrongs' I'd like you to ask your intuition:

Why is this behaviour perfect for me?

These are the sorts of things my clients have come up with in the past:

My partner buys things we don't need and clutters up the house with them . . .

. . . *but I love that my partner is so childlike and excitable about new gadgets and gizmos. It makes my life more fun and light-hearted.*

My partner is really messy . . .

. . . *but I love that my partner has different values to me and prefers getting out of the house to staying in. It means we have a great social life together.*

My partner wears clothes I don't like . . .

. . . *but I love that my partner doesn't care what people think — it's so liberated and sets a good example to me about the really important things in life.*

My partner doesn't earn much money . . .

. . . *but I love that my partner is more relationship-focused than career-focused. It means we have a wonderful, loving and communicative partnership.*

I don't want you to use this exercise to discount any genuine problems in your relationship. You know the ones I mean – unhealthy behaviour such as cheating, disrespect, not making any effort at all, emotional cruelty or indifference. But if you're in a healthy relationship, it's important to work with your psychic powers so you are projecting positive energy as often as you can. This means thinking the best of your partner and remembering why they're perfect for you.

As long as you're feeling positive about your partner inside, you will project a healthy, happy, positive energy into your psychic aura that continually builds love in your relationship. Without saying or doing anything, you will be working to create a loving, caring partnership. Remember, perfection doesn't exist. But 'perfect for you' does.

The Girls Who Wanted Perfection

There's nothing wrong with demanding perfection in your partner – if you don't mind staying single. How often have I heard successful, attractive people say that they are looking for a 'perfect' partner? Many, many times. And do you know what these people always have in common? They are single. People in happy relationships know that perfection isn't the goal. The goal is love and happiness.

I remember not so long ago talking to a group of girls in their late twenties who were a really dynamic and successful bunch and also very attractive. All five of them were saying that they couldn't believe that after all these years they were still single. Looking at them, you would indeed wonder why. These women were stunningly good-looking, had high-flying careers, enjoyed good social lives and generally lived life to the full.

However, they were all very particular about the sorts of men they would date. They wanted, in their words, 'perfection'. Rich, handsome, healthy, sporty men with no emotional baggage . . . the list went on. Now there's nothing wrong with visualizing what you want in a partner. But these girls weren't doing that. They wanted perfection in a man, not because they thought the 'perfect' qualities they required would make them happy, but because their egos demanded it. They wanted men who were exactly like them.

I said to them, perhaps not so tactfully, 'Is it any wonder you're all still single if you're looking for "perfection" instead of "perfect for you"?'

I felt very strongly that although these girls were outwardly successful, really they were projecting negativity. 'Not good enough' is a negative way to think and I could sense a real emotional block in the energy around them.

Instead of looking at a man and seeing what was wrong with him, I recommended they looked at what was right with him instead.

I explained to these girls that when you look for 'perfection' you send negative energy, because what you're really doing is focusing on who isn't good enough for you. Instead, I suggested they start looking for 'perfect for me'. This, I told them, would send out a much healthier and more positive psychic message. Instead of looking at a man and seeing what was wrong with him, I recommended they looked at what was right with him instead. I asked them to try out this attitude, which I knew would send out a much better energy of attraction, and report back to me in six months' time.

Six months later, four out of the five girls had met someone new and were in relationships. And they were happy. Their partners matched them well and brought out their best sides. The one girl who remained single was adamant she wanted to hold out for the 'very best', but of course the truth was that whilst she was projecting 'not good enough' energy, that was exactly what she would continue to attract.

Keeping the Psychic Sparkle

When you and your partner first met, things were new and exciting. Even if you'd already known each other for a while before you got together, the newness of a romantic relationship is always exhilarating and fresh. Two psychic energies blending together create positive sparks and fireworks that make life feel pretty wonderful.

As couples become closer and begin sharing their lives together, their energies often become more and more entwined until it's difficult to sense where one energy begins and another ends. There is simply one energy, which is all very nice and cosy, but it doesn't sparkle. A relationship is kept lively by ensuring that, although couples' energies are blended together, there is still enough difference between the two individuals to create sparks.

To keep a vibrant love in your relationship, you have to make sure your psychic aura is strong and clear so that you and your partner don't become bored and your relationship doesn't become routine. This means you have to carry on with your own interests and hobbies, and see your own friends independently of your partner. But, more importantly, you have to periodically get in touch with your higher self and remember who you are and what makes you the unique, independent and happy person your partner fell in love with. You can do this by keeping a higher-self diary.

The Higher-Self Diary

When was the last time you really talked to yourself? Your *true* self? We all have different personalities and opinions we wear throughout the day as we connect with different people in different environments. This is fine, but it's important to remember to come back to your true self, the higher self that brings you psychic messages, when you come home to your partner at the end of the day. This is especially true if your partner has a very strong energy, as you need to make sure you are communicating with your own true energy, and not your partner's energy, in order to maintain your independence and create a happy, stimulating relationship.

So I'd like you to periodically have conversations with your higher self to make sure you're still in touch with your own, unique psychic energy. It's OK – I won't be asking you to talk out loud and have everyone thinking you're a crazy person. What I'd like you to do is keep a diary – a very special diary in which you check in with and talk to your higher self.

Diary writing is something human beings have done for centuries. Have you ever wondered why? I believe it's because we all have a need to talk to ourselves, our *true* selves, in order to stay connected with our psychic side and our intuitive powers. And it's really the simplest thing in the world to do. Go out and buy yourself a nice notepad, one that's beautifully covered and inspires you to pick it up, find a quiet spot and write in it for at least twenty minutes. What should you write? Anything you like. You are having a conversation with your psychic self, the true self that really understands you, so nothing is off limits – no matter how trivial, negative or 'wrong'. This is your space to be totally, completely honest. To reveal everything from your inner soul. This could be petty moans and gripes about your partner or life in general, feelings about your body or your state of health or a little description of how the sun is shining on your desk. You needn't try and make sense from one moment to the next – just write whatever you like and feel how the more you scribble away, the closer and closer you are getting to you and your true, higher self.

> *Enjoy connecting with your psychic self in this way and I promise your relationship will be more benefits.*

I'd love you to write in your psychic diary every day, but I know real life is fast-paced, so checking in a few times a week is fine. It won't be a chore, I promise you. Once you get in the habit, it'll be a relief to talk to your psychic self and get all those niggles, worries and problems off your chest. Whilst you're talking to the real you, you'll also have amazing insights and revelations. Problems will become smaller and solutions will come thick and fast. Enjoy connecting with your psychic self in this way and I promise your relationship will see the benefits.

As your relationship continues to grow and thrive, remember to carry on using your intuition. It's there to help you stay happy, loved and fulfilled – just remember to use it!

Conclusion: Why Your Future Holds True Love

What is the key to finding true love? Looking within. Many people look outside themselves when they think about relationships and romance, but the secret of finding true love is to look within and discover your own gifts and powers.

After decades of psychic love counselling, I'm more sure than ever that true love lies in the future of everyone who looks for it. I've counselled thousands of clients over the years, many of whom have been quite certain that true love will never come into their lives. But after a few months (and sometimes weeks) of psychic training I've seen those very same people meet wonderful partners and soulmates who complete them and offer loving, committed relationships.

Clients have come to me on the verge of emotional breakdowns after years of dating disasters, or on their second or third divorce, or after having experienced yet another relationship break-up, and they've truly believed there is no hope for them when it comes to love. I've had the pleasure of seeing those heartbroken people settle down with truly wonderful partners and I have every confidence that you will do the same. I know for absolute certain that by tuning into your intuition and working with your psychic powers, you will bring true love into your life. Your soulmate is waiting for you – all you have to do is practise your psychic powers and listen to your instincts. The perfect partner is truly on his way.

When you start tuning into your intuition and unlocking your psychic powers, you'll find that the world changes in the most amazing and beneficial ways. You'll feel better about yourself, have more trust in your decisions and really open up a whole new world of wisdom and support. But you must practise. Don't give up, even if you have 'off' days when nothing seems to work and your judgement always seems wrong. Keep going, keep trying and eventually psychic abilities will be second nature. Remember what I told you at the beginning of the book? Practice makes psychic.

> *By tuning into your psychic self, you are accessing*
> *the real you, the confident, happy and loving you.*

As your psychic powers begin to grow, remember that good intuition isn't about tricking anyone or being selfish. You must use your powers for the greater good or you'll soon find yourself at odds with your intuition. Help your friends by using your intuition to suss out their love matches and always be polite and courteous to the people you date, even if your psychic alarm bells are going off and you know things won't work out. Remember – they need love and respect just like you do.

Over the years, I've found the biggest block to finding true love is self-esteem. Often clients contact me because they just don't think very much of themselves. Intuitively they know this is blocking their love life. Perhaps they've been dumped or treated badly, or perhaps they're from a family where love and respect weren't around very much. But for whatever reason, they're not feeling good and this is exactly what they project to others. They may dress attractively and act confidently, but low self-esteem can be so easily read by others as it sends off a very potent energy that blocks love and romantic progress.

By tuning into your psychic self, which is your higher, loving self and your inner wisdom, you are accessing the real you, the confident, happy and loving you. This inner voice is always full of love and praise, knows what a wonderful person you truly are and that your destiny is to find a perfect partner. The more you seek out this kind, caring voice the better you'll feel and the more you'll remove love blocks from your life.

I hope you're excited to think about the wonderful relationship you're about to embark on – it is a relationship with your true soulmate, and one that will love and nourish you for the rest of your life.

During this book, I've taught you many different tricks and techniques for clearing your mind and tuning into your intuition. Now it's time to take everything you've learned and make your life better. I want you to boost your confidence and your powers of attraction, visualize the perfect partner, avoid the 'Mr Wrongs', enjoy dating, have fun and find your soulmate . . . and you will.

Clients are always coming back to me when they've found their perfect man and telling me their stories, and I'd love to hear from you too. You can write to me at Jo@askthepsychic.co.uk and tell me all about your dating happiness, or even your dating disasters if you're still getting the hang of things.

I hope you're ready to experience all the other miraculous, positive things that come about when you tune into your higher wisdom.

So how are you feeling? Are you ready to start living a new sort of life – a life that makes full use of your psychic powers and inner wisdom? A life that's full of happiness and hope, rather than humiliation and confusion? A life in which you meet your perfect partner, rather than a series of dating disasters? Good. I hoped you would be.

I must leave you now to do the best you can with the advice and techniques in this book. I have every confidence that with practice and determination you'll not only find true love, but begin creating miracles in your life. Once you start connecting with your psychic side, you'll experience powerful visions and be able to literally write your own happy future. I hope you're ready for love to sweep you off your feet, and to experience all the other miraculous, positive things that come about when you tune into your higher wisdom.

Remember that you can do it. We have psychic abilities within us – it's just a case of practising, believing in our abilities and trusting that over time we'll start creating our own very special sort of magic. I believe very strongly that you are capable, confident and able to use intuition to find true love. You will do it. Trust me, but above all trust yourself.

With light and love, Joanna Scott